TALKING

BACK

TO

POEMS:

*A Working Guide for
the Aspiring Poet*

DANIEL ALDERSON

CELESTIALARTS

Berkeley, California

CELESTIAL ARTS PUBLISHING
P.O. Box 7123
Berkeley, CA 94707

Cover and text by Greene Design

Printed in the United States

Dedicated to my students.

Library of Congress Cataloging-in-Publication Data

Alderson, Daniel.
    Talking back to poems : a working guide for the aspiring poet /
    Daniel Alderson.
       p. cm.
    Includes bibliographical references (p.).
    ISBN 0-89087-795-5
    1. Poetry—Authorship. 2. Creative writing. I. Title.
PN1059.A9A43 1996
808.1—dc20   95-39441
                                           CIP

Contents

Preface

To *talk back* to a poem means to get active and write. Although writing clarifies the mind, too many writers are, for lack of discipline or inspiration, armchair writers. Most people resist the demands of using their minds to write because they do not find it to be rewarding. But writing poetry is rewarding; I say this confidently, based on my own experience as a writer and on the experiences of my students. When you talk back to the poems in this book, you become a poet practicing the craft. In the process, you deepen and enrich your experience of poetry.

Talking Back to Poems asks you to write poetry in response to other poetry. It provokes you to pick up a pen or go to a keyboard. It directs you to put your thoughts into concrete form, that is, to put words onto the printed page. The assumption underlying each prompt in *Talking Back to Poems* is that active engagement is grease to the wheel of learning. As an activity, reading is all to the good, but the usual kind of reading is passive compared to what poetry requires. Poetry, whether you are reading it or writing it, demands a highly engaged and active mind.

Talking Back to Poems is built upon the idea that when you use brilliant poems as prompts for your own writing, you are rewarded with clearer, more precise thinking and sharper, more incisive poems. The process of *Talking Back to Poems* moves you in a creative, constructive direction, enhancing not only your artistry with words but also your understanding of yourself and how you use words to make sense out of life.

Confidence in writing is a powerful thing. *Talking Back to Poems* acts as a catalyst for success in your practice of poetry. It works in the way that training wheels help you to build confidence on a bicycle, except that each new poem is a new vehicle full of new possibilities.

Think and behave like a poet practicing the craft. Be neither a recipient of some special knowledge nor a spectator of some distant fiction. Be an active maker of *meaning*. Push yourself to become a confident and expressive shaper of language. Don't take poetry sitting down. Stand up and write!

PART ONE:
Tools

CHAPTER ONE

Get Active As A Maker Of Meaning

READ, THINK, WRITE

You cannot "read" *Talking Back to Poems* in any satisfactory or self-improving sense of the word. When you simply read, you simply receive meaning; but when you pick up a pen, you stop holding poetry at arm's length. By accepting the challenge to write a poem in response to a poem, you coalesce the processes of reading, thinking and writing into one experience and bring it to life.

Talking Back to Poems begins with an Introduction but quickly pushes you toward writing your own version of this book. Chapters Two through Five cover four areas of "noticing" that my students and I use in looking at poems, namely, *Sound, Imagery, Structure* and *Meaning*. These areas are not intended to exclude each other or any other ideas about poetry. Rather, they are simply four ways to observe the craft behind the poem. This method of observation or of "noticing" allows each poem to reveal itself.

Talking back to a poem means writing a new poem of your own which echoes the poem you are reading and working with. You don't need to feel that you "understand" the poems which are used as prompts. Rather, do only one thing and do it with an active and open mind: notice things about each new poem. Notice things which are interesting or which are puzzling; notice things which seem curious or which seem very obvious.

It only makes sense that, when you're reading a poem for the first time, you're not likely to "understand" the poem in any complete or even meaningful sense; it would be more surprising if you did understand it fully on the first reading, given poetry's compressed and often purposely cryptic forms of expression.

However, you can read any poem in *Talking Back to Poems* and notice something interesting or insightful about it. You observe, you notice, you reflect: these become the basis of your new poem's echo of the original. This continuous, inter-connected process of reading, thinking and writing is at the heart of *Talking Back to Poems*.

NOTICE THINGS

Poets manipulate words for meaning and effect, and they do so by means of *sound, imagery, structure* and *meaning*. Sound is the raw substance of poetry, that which gives it its sculpted quality. Imagery refers to mental pictures and other information from the five senses and is especially close to the sensations of memory and dream. Structure includes all the ways in which poets give a sense of literal form and "architecture" to their poetry. Meaning designates the particular ways in which poems make meaning, and form a bridge between concrete perception and abstract understanding.

Sound is the "stuff" of poetry, adding a textural quality to the bare meanings of words. This is the quality of language that Greeks called onomatopœia: the "making of words" whose sounds are themselves suggestive of meaning. Consider the following excerpt of a poem by Dylan Thomas, *When All My Five and Country Senses See*. Read the lines in terms of the way the poet crafts sound:

> Love in the frost is pared and wintered by,
> The whispering ears will watch love drummed away
> Down breeze and shell to a discordant beach,
> And, lashed to syllables, the lynx tongue cry
> That her fond wounds are mended bitterly.
> My nostrils see her breath burn like a bush.
>
> ∾ *Dylan Thomas*

Sound, specifically the sound of words, is what a poet sculpts. Notice the way Thomas repeats sounds, not only within lines but sweeping across lines. Notice how the sounds of "w" and "b" are repeated in short bursts, seemingly dropped by the poet at one point and then brought back and developed further. Note how strong the "b" sound is in the last two lines: ". . . bitterly./. . . breath burn like a bush." Make the "b" sound three times with any enthusiasm and you will feel the force of this sound. In Dylan Thomas's poetry (or anyone else's) sound is not everything but sound is important and is observable. If you read a poem and you hear something— a pattern or a suggestive detail of sound—you are noticing an important aspect of the poet's craft.

Imagery is used by the poet to exploit the many possible mental associations and sensory images drawn to the mind by words. Notice how the imagery in Yvor Winter's poem, *By The Road To The Air-Base* creates a mental picture of a specific place by describing many small details and by triggering particular associations of sight and sound:

> The highway, like a beach,
> Turns whiter, shadowy, dry:
> Loud, pale against the sky,
> The bombing planes hold speech.
>
> Yet fruit grows on the trees;
> Here scholars pause to speak;
> Through gardens bare and Greek,
> I hear my neighbor's bees.
>
> ～ *Yvor Winters*

The plane screeches overhead. The noise of the engines is deafening, like a fast-forwarded train. Your feeling of Winter's "place" by the road to the air-base is whole and intense. Notice how Winter's poem uses imagery which is visual, as in "the highway . . . turns whiter, shadowy, . . . pale against the sky," and ". . . through gardens bare and Greek," as well as imagery of sound, as in "loud, . . . bombing planes hold speech" or "here scholars pause to speak," and ". . . I hear my neighbors bees." This is how a poet uses imagery to create a specific effect (one of seeing, hearing, sensing, or feeling a place) as these images and impressions from each of the five senses stimulate your imagination.

Structure is everywhere in poetry; sometimes it is hidden beneath the surface and sometimes it is obvious and overt. Rhyme schemes and page layout are tools used by the poet to create an architectural or literal form for the poem. One particular example of structure is rhyme scheme. Notice the enveloping pattern of Yvor Winter's two stanzas above, whose scheme is *abba cddc*. Page layout is another effective way to give structure to a poem. Notice it in the following short poem by John Tagliabue:

By a rich fast moving stream

I
saw
the
dragonfly
become a
dragon and
then a poem
about a dragonfly
becoming a dangerous
reader in fast pursuit
of summer transformations.

 ~ *John Tagliabue*

Tagliabue lays out the poem in the shape of a triangle. This creates a graphic tension which is suggestive, but difficult at first to account for. Tagliabue's poem uses its visual structure as a means to link images and ideas as they flow across the page. Notice the near absence of punctuation: there is one capital, "I," and one punctuation mark, a period. Notice that there are no rhymes, nor much alliteration. *By a rich fast moving stream* is a poem which is concentrated on its imagery, precisely by way of its structure. In fact, the way the poem's triangular shape draws attention to itself—is insistent in making itself into a recognizable, noticeable fact—serves its purpose by keeping you mindful of it as poetry. Further, the shape of the poem encourages the reader to slide down the poem quickly, becoming "the dangerous reader" Tagliabue describes.

Meaning is an overworked word for one of the things that poetry can make, namely, figurative meaning. Figurative meaning is any meaning which depends on the mind making a connection between an object and a secondary meaning. Some of the observable ways in which poems create meaning include metaphor, simile, analogy, irony, apposition, and rhetorical logic. These terms are explained in the glossary; however, as one example of the figurative use of language, consider *The Bath Tub* by Ezra Pound:

As a bathtub lined with white porcelain,

    When the hot water gives out or goes tepid,

    So is the slow cooling of our chivalrous passion,

O my much praised but-not-altogether-satisfactory

    lady.

    ~ *Ezra Pound*

The phrase "our love is like a bathtub of hot water" is a simile. It is also a good example of rhetorical logic, where syntactical markers give the poem its structure and underlying logic. Notice how important to Pound's meaning are the two words "as" and "so" in lines 1 and 3. Here, meaning is made by using signpost or directional words in order to draw a connection between two things. In the poem by Pound, the bathtub is very much a concrete object, whereas love, or "chivalrous passion," is pure abstraction. By pairing bathtub and love, Pound leads us to make a connection of meaning between them which animates the bathtub and reveals the nature of passion in love.

Permutation may be infinite in poetry, but underlying nearly any meaning or effect that can be noticed is the idea that the poet, in the practice of the poet's craft, makes a conscious use of sound, imagery, structure and meaning while writing.

GO TO WORK

At this juncture, you are encouraged to begin talking back to poems yourself. Rather than read this book straight through, you should proceed on your own: obtain a notebook, a blank book or whatever you are going to use for your written work and get going. You know enough to start now and will pick up the ideas behind *Talking Back to Poems* more quickly and more meaningfully if you take the time, after finishing this chapter, to do some of the Talk Back poems before reading the rest of the book.

At the least, you should do the first two or three prompts in each of the four sections: *Sound, Imagery, Structure* and *Meaning*. These prompts are short, directed and easy to work with. Each section builds toward longer and more complex poems. All of the prompts in these first four sections include some suggestions about how you might talk back to it. The prompts in the last section of *Talking Back to Poems* do not have these suggestions, so you are entirely on your own except for the three basic steps of "copying by hand," "writing what you notice," and "writing a poem of your own in response." By then, you won't need any additional help.

Obtain a notebook or journal or whatever works for you. This notebook is for copying the poems by hand and doing the draft revision work for your own Talk Back poems. Read the following instructions carefully, so that you are sure you have a basic understanding of how to write Talk Back poems. Your "writing process" should be as follows:

1) Copy the poem by hand. This process allows you to internalize the poem, to drink it in in its most minute detail in a way that reading never does. Try to keep your poem's line breaks, punctuation, and layout just like the original's. Although it may be boring and you might be tempted to skip it, copying by hand is extremely important because it makes you notice it.

2) Write what you notice about the poem. This step scratches at the surface of a poem's *meaning.* "Noticing" can take the form of any kind of marking on the page: you may wish to scan a poem, make note of its rhyme scheme, underline passages that resonate, draw circles and lines showing patterns or connections. Any marking or scribbling that prods or pokes the poem will help you talk back to it.

3) Using the draft revision process, write a poem of your own which echoes the original poem in some noticeable way. Start with a word, an image, or an idea—start with whatever enables you to start. Lean on the poem to which you are talking back as much as you need to. Work at echoing only one or two aspects of a poem rather than, say, trying to achieve a demanding rhyme scheme, a rigorously logical conceit, and a satiric voice all in a single Talk Back poem.

4) Creating a book of Talk Back poems is a rewarding way to "publish" your work. I ask my students, once they have a collection of their own poems, to copy or paste them into a blank book so that the original poem is on the page facing the Talk Back poem. A bound collection of these Talk Back entries documents and celebrates your growth as a writer.

If you are like my students, after you have written two or three poems in this way, you get warmed up to the procedure of talking back to poems and make the process of reading, thinking about, and writing a poem your own. If you have further questions about the writing process, or if yours is stalled, read the Appendix on The Writing Process (p. 108). If you find a poem outside of this book that you want to talk back to, copy the poem into your notebook and proceed. When you are between poems, you may wish to return to this Introduction and review the four ways of noticing things about poems. Create an on-going project.

Talking Back to Poems is not so much a book as it is a classroom, one in which the student/writer is placed at the center of learning. I say to students, "Gentle breath of yours my sails/ must fill, or else my project fails." In other words, unless you infuse this project with your own effort, I am not challenging you as I would like and you are not impelled to grow. Remember, a poem does not engage your literal-mindedness in the way that prose does. Prose is the language you would commonly hear at the grocery store or the doctor's office. Poetry on the other hand is the noisy silence of the rain-forest, full of mystery and the unknown. There are uncomfortable feelings in poetry, for you do not have the conventions of Standard Written English to comfort you.

This is why it is so important to work actively while writing poetry: it helps, when stiff, to get up and move around; it helps, when trying to make sense of a poem, to use the methods of the poet in order to make your own meaning. Put this book down now and go begin writing on your own.

CHAPTER TWO

Sound

HEAR WHAT YOU SEE

To begin our first discussion of sound, a disclaimer must immediately be put forth: namely, it is important to remember that none of these ways of noticing things about poems is in anyway intended to exclude another. On the contrary, the best poems are typically masterful in all of these ways.

It is nevertheless true that some poems rely more heavily on sound to achieve an effect, just as some poems rely more heavily upon imagery, structure or figurative meaning. The work of Samuel Taylor Coleridge, for example, reveals a fascination with the ways in which the sounds of the words themselves carry currents and cross-currents of meaning beneath the obvious surface of a poem.

Coleridge's *Kubla Khan* is a very musical poem, but notice, as you read the following excerpt, that no instruments are actually playing. Instead, Coleridge weaves a spell of sounds in your ear and in your imagination:

> Could I revive within me
>
> Her symphony and song,
>
> To such a deep delight 'twould win me,
>
> That with music loud and long,
>
> I would build that dome in air,
>
> That sunny dome! Those caves of ice!
>
> And all who heard should see them there.

> ∼ *Samuel Taylor Coleridge*

Notice how each line ends with an open sound. Read the lines over again and as you come to the end of each line of the poem, observe the position of your mouth. Given the fact that all of these sounds are also used as line end-rhymes, they stand out and even seem to have a movement of their own:

...me

...song

...me
...long
...air
...ice
...there

This arrangement of sounds at the end of each line yields a sense of antici-
pation which moves from one line to the next, reinforcing a feeling of sus-
pense by causing each line to end in an open-mouthed and unresolved way.

Notice, too, the lack of metrical symmetry as Coleridge passes
smoothly from the first two lines, which have three stressed, or accented,
syllables, to the rest of the passage, in which each line has four syllables
that are accented. The poem's heart seems to skip a beat and to change
rhythm, but it occurs beneath the surface of the poem. The rhyme scheme
wraps over the change in meter like a poetic hinge, holding the two sepa-
rate pieces of poem together and contiguous.

IMAGINE RATS

Sound is also one of the essential elements in *The Hollow Men* by T.S. Eliot.
The heart of the poem's meaning is entangled in its thoroughly enchanting
and distracting patterns of sound. The following excerpt from *The Hollow
Men* is not meant to stand for the whole poem, but rather is an example of
something that can be noticed about sound. In it, Eliot is describing "the
hollow men:"

Our dried voices, when
We whisper together
Are quiet and meaningless
As wind in dry grass
Or rats' feet over broken glass
In our dry cellar

    ~ *T.S. Eliot*

The voice of the "hollow men" is created by the resonance between sound
and imagery. As only one example of this, consider the progression of
sounds in the following phrase: "rats' feet over broken glass." The sounds
"rts," "ft," "vrt," "brkn," and "gls" require careful enunciation and in their

overall effect are sliding and close-mouthed. The line brings to the ear the disquieting sound of intrusion and it brings to the mind's eye an image of abandonment and vacancy.

Notice the structure of the end-rhyme sounds beginning with line 5 and the way in which they form an *abbba* rhyme scheme. Notice also the fact that "together" and "dry cellar" form an unmistakable slant rhyme. "Grass" and "glass" rhyme in a repetition of sound which clashes with the other rhymes in this section of the poem, most of which are slant rhymes. Eliot is careful to avoid committing himself to any metrical pattern. In fact, the way the poem darts from one invented form to another suggests a skittish, erratic, stop-and-start movement, not unlike "wind in dry grass/ or rats' feet over broken glass..." themselves. This is an example, broadly speaking, of onomatopœia.

Onomatopœia is a wizened, slightly comic word, but it is an ancient and interesting one. The last part, "pœia," has the same root as "poet." To the Greeks, this root word, "pœia," meant "maker" or "shaper," where there is a great awareness of craft. In poetry, attention is paid to all aspects of words and the ways in which they are put together, yielding insight that is grasped for an instant, the imprint of which remains forever.

GO AND CATCH A FATHER

The poem from which the following excerpted stanza is taken, *Song* by John Donne, argues that finding a woman who is "true" is an impossible task and an absurd notion. But there is something in the first stanza which goes far beyond this underlying idea:

> Go and catch a falling star,
>> Get with child a mandrake root,
> Tell me, where all past years are,
>> Or who cleft the Devil's foot,
> Teach me to hear mermaids singing,
>> Or to keep off envy's stinging,
>>> And find
>>> What wind
> Serves to advance an honest mind.

> ⁓ *John Donne*

Donne seems to be swept away by the sheer force of sound. Consider first the end rhymes, which form an *ababccddd* pattern. Notice, too, the shift from the first four masculine rhymes to two double-ringing feminine rhymes, then returning to masculine rhyme in the three final ending-sounds:

...star
...root
...are
...foot
...stinging
...singing
...find
...wind
...mind

The slant rhymes ("root" and "foot," "wind" and "mind"), which may have been true rhymes when Donne spoke them, are very disarming in the way their exact sounds differ now. The fact that these words have identical spellings makes them true sight rhymes as well as slant rhymes.

The first words of each of the lines also have a rhyming and logic among them. Consider,

Go...
    Get...
Tell...
    Or...
Teach...
    Or...
       find...
       what...
Serves...

This is a strong, forceful rhetoric: verbs in the present tense directly telling you what to do. The sentence structure is repeated five times in "go," "get," "tell," "teach," and "find," all of which are commands. This pattern is continued even when the line-length undergoes a sharp change.

Perhaps the most striking aspect of this poem's sound is in the rhythm of the last three lines: two short lines of only one beat, and a last line which runs on to four deep and even-toned beats (/^^/^/^/). If you read just the last three or four lines of the passage over again, you can see the way in which the arrested line-spacing, together with the overlapping true and slant rhymes, gives movement and breath to the ideas being conveyed by the poem.

One of my students, Lily Liang, chose to talk back to this passage by John Donne. She writes on the subject of war, and the seeming impossibility of stopping it forever:

WAR

Run and destroy the hourglass,

    Stop the passing of the sands of time,

Tell me how long this nightmare will last,

    Or how many innocent victims will die.

Help me stop the endless tears from falling,

    Or prevent the world from darkening,

        And find

        The unkind

Cowards who left the pain and anguish in my mind.

~ *Lily Liang*

Besides creating a remarkable Talk Back poem, Lily does two things which are equally interesting. First, she changes the conceit. A conceit is the figurative construct upon which a poem's logic rests. She changes it from Donne's "A true woman is impossible to find" to her own "The ending of war is impossible," the later of which seems darker and more worldly. Second, notice how much of the sound structure she managed to retain, especially the end-rhymes. She uses rhythmic tension to add a layer of meaning to the words by altering the rhythm of Donne's last three lines.

Jenny Hau, another student, chose to talk back to the same poem. Her poem explores the father's role in the family and offers him some advice:

A REAL FATHER

Run and find a new father,
    Get a man who cares for his son,
Tell him to save your mother
    Or to defeat the evil one,
Teach him to love a woman,
Not to be a careless man,
    And love
    What's above
Him to treasure what a family is made of.

    ~ *Jenny Hau*

Notice how her rhymes move artfully between true and slant. The words father and mother with their "th" sound are a weak slant rhyme. However, when juxtaposed prominently, they resonate for obvious reasons of association and training.

Note the direct clarity of lines five and six, and the way the inherent sound quality of "woman" and "man" produces a strong effect. Finally, the sharp syntactical slap around the corner after line 8 represents an example of why, occasionally, one is compelled to break the pattern one has chosen to imitate.

SPEAK WELL, QUIETLY

One of the many ways of talking about a poem's sound is to speak of its voice. By voice we mean the writer's voice, which, to the extent that we "hear" it, wins us over into its confidence. All writers are concerned with voice, and it tends to be recognized first by the reader. For example, many students, reading Josephine Miles' poem, *The Faith,* are moved to echo her quiet, well-spoken voice:

THE FAITH

Sir, take this faith, it will do you no harm.
It is mine and sits on your shoulder.
It will not chatter.

It will take pleasure in seeing you move,
You are hesitant and placid and that is a good motion,
And faith is a good devotion.

Sir, do not refuse one's stranger companiment,
It will insist by no sign or pressure,
And will have measure.

~ *Josephine Miles*

The sounds of the "middle way," or of least resistance, convey restraint. Notice the end-rhymes which are slanted and feminine. They give a clipped and well-mannered quality to the poem, and reinforce its polite, genteel tone.

When you read *The Joy*, a poem by Peter Yee which talks back to *The Faith*, notice the way in which the key phrases are altered to brighten his tone. He holds onto the feeling of intimacy, yet gives the poem his own strong voice:

THE JOY

Ma'am, take this joy, it will keep you happy.
It was mine and will be with you now.
It is respectful and will bow.

It will enjoy being with you.
You are startled, frightened and that's a bad feeling
But joy is healing.

Ma'am, do not refuse its friendship.
It is not dangerous,
But is generous.

~ *Peter Yee*

Peter responds to *The Faith* on several levels at once with sound. Notice how he has used the original poem as a template, incorporating the same elements of varied line lengths, end-rhymes which are feminine and slant, stanzas of three lines with the last two lines rhyming, truncated third lines, and an insistent and intense voice.

Most of us when working on our own would probably shy away from ending each line of verse with a true rhyme because we have been taught that it is unsophisticated. Yet many passionate, articulate poems from the history of English literature are written with true rhymes. Phyllis Wheatley's use of rhyming couplets identifies her as a seventeenth century poet; but if you consider her rhyme scheme and meter as the standard conventions of her time, it is clear that she transcends these formal aspects:

ON BEING BROUGHT FROM AFRICA TO AMERICA

'Twas mercy brought me from my *Pagan* land,
Taught my benighted soul to understand
That there's a God, that there's a *Saviour* too:
Once I redemption neither sought nor knew.
Some view our sable race with scornful eye,
"Their colour is a diabolic die."
Remember, *Christians, Negroes,* black as *Cain,*
May be refin'd, and join th' angelic train.

～ *Phyllis Wheatley*

When Clarissa Chiu chose to talk back to Wheatley's poem, she naturally gravitated toward the end-rhymes to give focus and intensity to her poem. Notice, however, how she rejects Wheatley's meter, allowing her more room for natural phrasing:

ON PRIDE

Yes, I agree and understand

It was mercy that brought you from your pagan land.

You know why? Cause that's what I went through.

I believed that there was a God for me too.

Some are mean, and yet some do try.

At the end though, they still manage to make us cry.

My friend, we're all on the same road, in the same game.

Never retaliate and never forget your name.

~ *Clarissa Chiu*

This is a powerful response to a powerful poem, and it demonstrates a masterful sensitivity to the sounds of language. She echoes the *aabbccdd* rhyme scheme and the natural cadence and tone of the spoken word. There is a specific, logical development which echoes Wheatley's poem in that they both have a moral ending. Clarissa shows what it means to talk back to a poem using sound as the main way of echoing the original.

CHAPTER THREE
Imagery

PICTURE ORANGE

If sound is the visceral, kinesthetic force in poetry, imagery is the cerebral, imaginative one. For example, if you close your eyes and picture orange, this is the level of thought where imagery thrives. This state of mind is close to dreaming, and the loose associations involved can be very effective when crafted by the poet attuned to imagery. In the opening stanza of *Sunday Morning,* Wallace Stevens invites us to enter a visual world, a world of dream.

> She dreams a little, and she feels the dark
> Encroachment of that old catastrophe,
> As a calm darkens among water-lights.
> The pungent oranges and bright, green wings
> Seem things in some procession of the dead,
> Winding across wide water, without sound.
>
> ∿ *Wallace Stevens*

The poem asks us to imagine on the visual plane, "without sound," like a film strip or video with the sound turned off. Notice, Stevens uses no obvious rhymes at all. There is some notable assonance, especially with all those W's in the last line of the passage, but otherwise, it is a poem which avoids end-rhymes and metrical regularity.

Many of Stevens' poems rely heavily upon imagery. His *Thirteen Ways of Looking at a Blackbird* is a famous poem which suggests a series of snapshots, each a different point of view for the camera. Stevens avoids common or traditional *structures* of rhyme and meter, preferring instead spatial organizations. Stevens practiced a craft of imagery and page layout.

This is also true of Frank O'Hara. He achieves cadence, balance, and poise by using imagery and its associations in much the same manner as Stevens. The following passage is taken from *Why I am Not a Painter:*

…One day I am thinking of
a color: orange. I write a line
about orange. Pretty soon it is a
whole page of words, not lines.
Then another page. There should be
so much more, not of orange, of
words, of how terrible orange is
and life.

∼ *Frank O'Hara*

It is difficult to say what exactly orange means in this poem. Yet orange remains vivid in our imagination throughout because it is color. The color orange, which we know as a color used in visual art, is used as an ironic vehicle to carry the idea that O'Hara is a poet and not a painter.

Notice how O'Hara adheres to what might be easily imagined in the mind. The self-consciousness of this method promotes a reflective, meditative state of mind. There are no smells, no sweaty palms, no pounding hearts. There is only one abstraction, one image so concrete and so palpable it is made to symbolize everything which makes it impossible for O'Hara to be a painter and impossible for him not to be a poet.

James Wright is another poet who, although he "cannot" be a painter, is often highly visual with his poetry. Notice how the following poem, *Spring Images,* is organized around its imagery:

SPRING IMAGES
Two athletes
Are dancing in the cathedral
Of the wind.

A butterfly lights on the branch
Of your green voice.

Small antelopes
Fall asleep in the ashes
Of the moon.

∼*James Wright*

Although sound and structure are important to the overall effect of this poem, it is the imagery that asks to be noticed. There is a quiet which descends on Wright's poem—like the quiet of meditation, or that of complete attention. It descends, too, on Lily Liang's poem, which talks back to Wright's *Spring Images:*

SUMMER

Willow trees
Are whispering softly to the soul
Of the earth

Ladybugs decorate the dusty ground
Of the secluded trails

Glittering stars
light up the playground
Of the heavens

～ *Lily Liang*

The uncanny thing about this poem is the way in which it adroitly avoids any gratuitous rhyme or meter, making the images stand for themselves. Her thought is one of precise imagery, clear and transparent. Although imagery is rarely used to the complete exclusion of all else, some poets, including many of the twentieth century, are so focused on achieving this kind of transparency, it is difficult not to "notice" their imagery.

William Carlos Williams is one such poet. He always seems to take his cat-like steps with excruciating patience and care. Indeed, his portrayal of old age in *To Waken An Old Lady* is found in the tentative, halting, and careful pace typical of much of his poetry:

TO WAKEN AN OLD LADY

Old age is
a flight of small
cheeping birds
skimming
bare trees

above a snow glaze.
Gaining and failing
they are buffeted
by a dark wind—
But what?
On harsh weedstalks
the flock has rested,
the snow
is covered with broken
seedhusks
and by the wind tempered
by a shrill
piping of plenty.

~ *William Carlos Williams*

This is a very spare style of writing, and it effectively conveys feeling without being overly emotional. Napat Chananudech in his Talk Back poem, *To Start A New Car*, also deftly uses this style.

To Start A New Car

A new car is
a breeze
of fresh air
blowing
smoothly into your nostrils.
Turning and learning
they are followed
by a blast of knowledge —
But What?
On easy flowing
comes a tornado,
Blowing dirt onto

continued on next page.

the mud-covered car
and it passes
leaving a hunger
for oil
and bank books.

     ∼ *Napat Chananudech*

Napat turns dirt into greed and hunger using imagery. Jenell Marshall took her Talk Back poem in an unpredictable direction. As you read it, notice the interesting ways in which she manages to both echo Williams's work and create a strikingly original poem:

TO ROCK A BABY TO SLEEP

birth is a
rosebud stung
by a wasp
weeping
by a pond
sprouting and blossoming
they are picked and torn
Why?

Old grey rabbits
nibbling while
sunbathing,
the grass is green
acorns scattered
from fallen
trees,
with wind hollering.

     ∼ Jenell Marshall

Although very different from Napat's *To Start A New Car,* Jenell Marshall's *To Rock A Baby To Sleep* captures the same stark, imagistic tone.

As the last of our examples of imagistic poems, Cecily Ina writes *The Darkness* as a poem in response to *The Cold Room* by Yvor Winters:

THE COLD ROOM

The dream
stands
in the night
above unpainted
floor and chair.

The dog is
dead asleep
and
will not move
for god or fire.

And from the
ceiling
darkness bends
a heavy flame.

~ *Yvor Winters*

THE DARKNESS

As I
speak
the words
roll off my
tongue, and
drift off.

continued on next page.

My mate
drifts slowly
off into an
endless
dream.

Then I reach
out for
someone
to grasp.
∼ *Cecily Ina*

CHAPTER FOUR

Structure

DRAW ENCHANTING LEAVES

Poems always have structure, obvious or not, and it is an important thing to notice even in its absence. Sometimes, structure is the one thing about a poem that really attracts our attention. Some poems structure themselves by means of what is literally heard, and some structure themselves by means of what is literally seen. The structures of hearing are mainly rhyme schemes or poetic forms, and these are based on very literal patterns of sound running through the lines, as well as on the repetition of sounds at the ends of lines.

A poem can also be structured visually, by means of its arrangement upon the printed page. Here, structure is created by the literal appearance of the printed words on the page rather than by the literal sound as in rhymed poems.

e.e. cummings is a master of the page-layout method of structuring poetry. He arranges his words as though their meanings could be put together like flowers in a vase or notes on the refrigerator. In other words, cummings is a poet who claims full spatial plasticity. In the following poem, squint your eyes and imagine you can't "read" any of the words; try to focus on the way they are arranged on the printed page. See if you can discover any design or "craft" in the way the words are placed.

IV

into the smiting

sky   tense

with

blend

ing

the

tree   leaps

continued on next page.

               a stiffened exquisite

i

wait the sweet
annihilation of swift
flesh

i make me stern against
your charming strength

O haste
               annihilator
drawing into you my enchanting
leaves

∿ *e.e. cummings*

A moment's reflection suggests that cummings's "stiffened exquisite" protrudes for a reason. As is typical in these kinds of observations, it is difficult to say exactly what this spatial disruption of the norm accomplishes. It is, however, quite easy to see how different this poem would be if it were put into standard written English: "Into the smiting sky, tense with blending, the tree leaps: a stiffened exquisite...." The poem's structural tension is relaxed and the language goes flat. Every poem is a created object, and poets like cummings use the page like a canvas, placing words upon it as if they were images themselves.

Kevin Agness talks back to *VII*, another poem by e.e. cummings, in a poem called *The Classroom*. Notice the way in which Kevin has chosen to both echo cumming's spatial organization and to mimic his rejection of stylistic convention, producing a similar grammar of physical, literal space:

VII

the rose
is dying the
lips of an old man murder

the petals
hush
mysteriously
invisible mourners move
with prose faces and sobbing, garments
The symbol of the rose

motionless
with grieving feet and
wings
mounts

against the margins of steep song
a stallion sweetness   ,the

lips of an old man murder

the petals.

~ *e.e. cummings*

THE CLASSROOM

the thought
is breathing past
minds of the learning few

the idea
gigantic
misunderstood by wondering eyes
questioning voices and wondering minds
the thought is left alone

continued on next page.

unwanted

it is sitting with

innovations

new ways

untouched

ignorance is bliss through the day
everyone left wondering,   the

minds of the learning few

the thought

~ *Kevin Agness*

e.e. cummings is of course not the only poet to concern himself primarily
with structure in poetry. For instance, Robert Frost confined his poetry to
rhyme schemes and metrical patterns which would make you old before
your time if you tried to duplicate them.

DROP WHEN YOU COME TO THE END

The poems of Robert Frost follow strict predetermined rhyme schemes
and use true rhymes and metrical regularity. Consider, for example, the fol-
lowing stanza from *The Oven Bird:*

The bird would cease and be as other birds
But that he knows in singing not to sing.
The question that he frames in all but words
Is what to make of a diminished thing.

~ *Robert Frost*

Although Frost could have served as a model for noticing a poem's sound,
he shows up here in our discussion of structure because he is so precise.
While many poets use sound effectively, even masterfully, few achieve
such succinct mastery in the tight metrical discipline required by these
four-lined stanzas. Most of Frost's poems are built from stanzas just like
this one.

One of the interesting effects of tightly configured stanzas, usually either *abab* or *aabb*, is their level of compression. Notice how much meaning and thought W.B. Yeats attains in the following stanza:

YOUTH AND AGE

Much did I rage when young,
Being by the world oppressed,
But now with flattering tongue
It speeds the parting guest.

~ *W.B. Yeats*

Youth and Age is a serious poem with a wry sensibility. The voice that creeps out from behind these elegant words does so with a sly, reluctant grin. The tautness of the poem's comic irony is made possible by its compressed structure.

Notice that the following Talk Back poems echo the original in very different, but equally valid, ways. Samson Gee, in his *Love and Marriage*, takes a hard look at some serious issues and creates a sense of urgency by his deft use of rhyme:

LOVE AND MARRIAGE

I have this big wish,
Wanting to spend my entire life
With the one I cherish,
By asking her, "Will you be my wife?"

~ *Samson Gee*

If Samson Gee's poem is expressive of his serious-mindedness, Chris Junkin's is equally expressive of his eagerness to find humor:

LOVE STOPS

The years make love funny
The courting game never ends
Sharing vows and money
The end will come when one drops.

~ *Chris Junkin*

"Drops" drops off the rhyme scheme by failing to rhyme with "ends." It does, however, fishhook onto the title like a brittle trout on the end of a line. When you consider the effect of this repeated sound it has a "ka-thump" which gives structure to the feelings of uncertainty expressed by the poem.

WORM INTO FLOWERS

As a final example of how structure might be noticed, consider *The Castle of Thorns* by Yvor Winters, which was chosen as a Talk Back prompt by Kirk Hieda. Kirk's poem, *The House of Flowers,* is in some ways an overly ambitious poem. It takes on both a formidable structure of end-rhymes, *abbacddc efgefg,* and the long English tradition of Sonnets. Kirk's poem is nevertheless an interesting and a commendable one:

THE CASTLE OF THORNS

Through autumn evening, water whirls thin blue,
From iron to iron pail—old, lined, and pure;
Beneath, the iron is indistinct, secure
In revery that cannot reach to you.
Water it was that always lay between
The mind of man and that harsh wall of thorn,
Of stone impenetrable, where the horn
Hung like the key to what it all might mean.

My goats step guardedly, with delicate
Hard flanks and forest hair, unchanged and firm,
A strong tradition that has not grown old.
Peace to the lips that bend in intricate
Old motions, that flinch not before their term!
Peace to the heart that can accept this cold!

∼ *Yvor Winters*

THE HOUSE OF FLOWERS

Through the days of Spring, the sky lights blue,
In soil and compost lain fresh and pure
Beneath the soil of the roots of fern
A revery that can reach you.
Water that always runs through
The sun, that harsh window
Of glass penetrable, where the willow
Grows steady and true.

The worms move smoothly, with delicate
Movement, long and brown,
Much love of the mind
That found the time
To do this.

~ *Kirk Hieda*

Kirk's *The House of Flowers,* discards the long lines and learned diction of Winters in favor of a leaner, more understated phrasing—so much so that the second section of the poem exits like a cat out the back door. Nevertheless, Kirk stays true to his own voice where he abandons Winter's rigorous formal demands. The result is an admirable poem that uses earthworms to reveal to us the source of flowers.

CHAPTER FIVE

Meaning

SEE THE SEVEN SIDES

The last way of noticing things about poems deals with the construction of figurative meaning. Many of the things which have been discussed up to this point are literal: literal sound, literal images in the mind, literal structures of form on the printed page. Here there is a shift from this relatively solid ground. Whenever you reach a place in a poem that moves you from concrete perception to abstract understanding, you know you are in the realm of figurative meaning.

Figurative meaning includes any literary or rhetorical strategy which has as its effect a clear connection between a known and unknown thing—something concrete and something abstract. Take the figurative construction or "figure" in the previous paragraph as an example: "Here there is a shift from this relatively solid ground." We have all walked on solid ground and have a strong, experience-based sense of it, so we know about solid ground. On the other hand, we have no sense at all of how we make the jump to figurative understanding. So we craft a metaphor which helps us think more clearly about it. In fact, it is the metaphor itself which carries understanding to a new place.

Carlos Drummond de Andrade practices this figurative craft in her poetry. Notice how the following excerpt from her *Seven-Sided Poem* puts all known and imaginable space into seven short lines:

Universe, vast universe,

if I had been named Eugene

that would not be what I mean

but it would go into verse

faster.

Universe, vast universe,

my heart is vaster.

~ *Carlos Drummond de Andrade*

Translated by Elizabeth Bishop

The specificity of the name Eugene strikes a sudden and unexpected pose. Bishop deflates her would-be romantic gesture sardonically, then elevates it again in a sweeping statement.

The first line, "universe, vast universe," is a figurative expression of longing or regret as it literally describes all known or imagined space. The passage might be paraphrased in this way: If I had been born a man, I could more easily imagine having said in words what I have to say; but what I have to say cannot be said by a man's words. And so she chooses these words, poetic ones with figurative meaning, in order to convey the idea.

Another poet who uses figurative language with the same facility is Derek Walcott. In the following excerpt from Walcott's poem, *The Harbour*, the "sea of love" is used as the central figurative device:

> Yet others who now watch my progress outward,
>
> On a sea which is crueler than any word
>
> Of love, may see in me the calm my passage makes,
>
> Braving new water in an antique hoax;
>
> And the secure from thinking may climb safe to liners
>
> Hearing small rumours of paddlers drowned near stars.

> ∾ *Derek Walcott*

Just as life at sea is unpredictable, Walcott seems to say that you cannot love and be safe. The unexpected ending also shows figurative language in action. Suddenly the seekers of safety have a place to retreat, as an ocean liner is a relatively safe place to be when at sea. However, the "secure from thinking," although aboard the ship, are still not "safe" from love.

These poems by Bishop and Walcott are both examples of poems which use figurative language to animate a many-sided understanding. Normally, in the urgency of daily life, you seek ways of understanding which are simple and workable; you are restrained and disciplined in your imaginative adventures by the needs of existence and survival. But in a poem, you are released from these constraints. The poem, when carefully crafted, prompts you to reach for complexity and depth in your understanding.

MAKE MEANING HAPPEN

When you are talking back to poems, you can use some of these same figurative constructions. Notice the way in which the following three student poems, Kathy Quach's *Rainbow*, Oliver Choy's *Weight*, and Johnson Lee's *Memo* all echo the figurative strategy used in *Note*, by the poet, William Stafford:

NOTE

straw, feathers, dust—
little things

but if they all go the same way,
that's the way the wind goes.

∼ *William Stafford*

RAINBOW

Orange, blue, yellow...
seven colors,

but if they all connect together,
that's the way the rainbow looks.

∼ *Kathy Quach*

WEIGHT

Anvil, paperclips, books—
Different weights,

But if you drop them from a high place
They land at the same time.

∼ *Oliver Choy*

MEMO
Pencil, paper, carbon copies:
Tools that move data;

But even with all of this,
Nothing happens at the office.

~ *Johnson Lee*

The figurative strategy here is straightforward: make a list of three simple, concrete objects; define them in the second line; skip a line and begin with "but." Then construct the last two lines so that these "things" are not what they seem—the beginning does not, somehow, predict the end and the whole is not like its parts. *Rainbow, Weight,* and *Memo* are all poems which use the word "but" as a central signpost indicating a distinction or a difference between one thing and another. The use of this rhetorical device helps reveal the tension between the nearsightedness of minutia and the broad sweep of imaginative vision.

MOVE THE GREAT SLOTH
Again, the subject is love, this time in the figure of a heart which is unreachable, immovable, and inscrutable:

A MAJOR WORK
Poems are hard to read
Pictures are hard to see
Music is hard to hear
And people are hard to love

But whether from brute need
Or divine energy
At last mind eye and ear
And the great sloth heart will move.

~ *William Meredith*

There are several things to notice about this poem beyond its figurativeness. First, it literally has a wall within it: a wall of space between the two stanzas, the two main parts of the poem. Second, the poem has a strong logical and syntactical drive. Consider the signpost words, the syntactical road markers:

    ____ are ____
    ____ are ____
    ____ is ____
    and ____ are ____

    but whether from ____
    or ____
    at last ____ ____ and ____
    and ____ will move.

Notice how this syntax is logical even without its content. Third but not least, there is an air of abstraction which is created by the phrase: "Poems are hard to read." This is literally true, but never are the words that describe it concrete or specific. Instead we are cajoled with: "At last mind eye and ear/ And the great sloth heart [our sloth heart] will move."

In Meredith's poem, *A Major Work,* the tone, the voice, and the atmosphere of abstraction all seem to come from someone hesitant about love. In other words, the language of the poem is specifically chosen to suggest someone slow to love—someone who is stuck, so to speak, in abstract language. Notice the way in which both of the following Talk Back poems echo Meredith's sense of distance and tentativeness:

HARD LIFE

Life is hard
Money is hard to make
Emotion is hard to tell
And hard to be human

But no matter from where
Once here
At last open mind
And the great knowledge comes into you

    ~ *Nha Ta*

AFTERWARDS

Life is impossible to bear
The past is impossible to erase
The pain is impossible to dull
Memories are impossible to forget

But whether for the sake of others to hear
Or ourselves to praise
We say we've retrieved our heart and soul
In full
And have nothing to regret.

～ *Lily Liang*

Nha and Lily both echo the rhetorical structure mapped out by Meredith in *A Major Work* in order to navigate their way through very different, but equally powerful, poems of their own.

VISUALIZE!

Frank O'Hara's poem serves as our last example of figurativeness. It has no obvious metaphors or similes, no rhymes or strict metrical pattern, but it does have a strong voice:

AUTOBIOGRAPHIA LITERARIA

When I was a child
I played by myself in a
corner of the schoolyard
all alone.

I hated dolls and I
hated games, animals were
not friendly and birds
flew away.

continued on next page.

If anyone was looking
for me I hid behind a
tree and cried out "I am
an orphan."

And here I am, the
center of all beauty!
writing these poems!
Imagine!

    ~ *Frank O'Hara*

I have always understood this poem to be highly ironic, and I still believe that irony was O'Hara's original intent. But Randolf Lu reads it differently, yet in a way that is very moving.

ANOTHER LITERARIA AUTOBIOGRAPHIA

When I was still young
I came with my family
to a great nation
called United States.

I didn't like the environment and I
didn't speak the language, people
were not friendly and they
walked away.

If I was called in
class I hid behind the
others and yelled out, "I don't
speak English."

But here I am, learning
This beautiful language!
Trying to write these poems!
Visualize!

~ *Randolf Lu*

Notice some of the things that Randolf holds onto. His is like O'Hara's poem in that it is intimate and personal. He mimics the movement of O'Hara's four "unstructured" quatrains by means of enjambment; he maintains its unpredictable, but perfectly recognizable, cadences of speech and phrasing. He even echoes O'Hara's irony in the poem: while the original is based upon the absurdity of the childish gesture which underlies some supposedly "serious" poetry, Lu's irony is based on the sheer unlikelihood that a baby born in China in 1977 would be talking back to poems in San Francisco in 1995.

The work of *Talking Back to Poems* is a way for you to move beyond the conventions of prose into the wilds of poetry. Like Lu and the others, you should be talking back to poems, too.

PART TWO:
Prompts

CHAPTER SIX:

Sound Prompts

THE STONE...

The stone is a mirror which works poorly.
Nothing in it but dimness. Your dimness or its dim-
ness, who's to say? In the hush your heart sounds
like a black cricket.

∽ *Charles Simic*

▲

1. Copy the poem by hand.

2. Charles Simic uses onomatopœia here. If you scan the flow of consonant
and vowel sounds you will notice a well marked phonetic progress, moving
from the initial m's and n's, and the "oo" and "ay" of "Who's to say," to sibi-
lants and shsh's, finally landing with the implosive "bla" sound and the dou-
ble click of "cricket."

3. Using the draft revision process, write a poem of your own repeating the
statement-question-statement form in a single short paragraph. Work to
create a progression of sounds which begin open, become more closed, and
then finally implode and cackle, echoing the sound of Simic's poem.

SONG
an excerpt

Go and catch a falling star,
    Get with child a mandrake root,
Tell me, where all the past years are,
    Or who cleft the Devil's foot,
Teach me to hear mermaids singing,
Or to keep off envy's stinging,
      And find
      What wind
Serves to advance an honest mind.

~ *John Donne*

▲

1. Copy the poem by hand.

2. Notice that the first six lines of the stanza are consistently iambic and that each has four accented beats. Notice also how the shortened line near the end of the stanza creates a tension, and the last line releases it by returning to the four-beat line.

3. Using the draft revision process, write a poem of your own which alternates between true rhyme and slant rhyme and mimics the broken metrical pattern of the last two lines. (See p. 17–9.)

THE FAITH

Sir, take this faith, it will do you no harm.
It is mine and sits on your shoulder.
It will not chatter.

It will take pleasure in seeing you move,
You are hesitant and placid and that is a good motion,
And faith is a good devotion.

Sir, do not refuse one's stranger companiment,
It will insist by no sign or pressure,
And will have measure.

～ *Josephine Miles*

▲

1. Copy the poem by hand.

2. Write what you notice about *The Faith*.

3. Write three, three-line stanzas in which the first two lines are noticeably longer than the shortened last line, and in which the second and third lines end in a slant, feminine rhyme. Write your poem so that it sounds as though it is being spoken in a quiet, reassuring voice.

WHEN LOVE MEETS LOVE

When love meets love, breast urged to breast,

God interposes,

An unacknowledged guest,

And leaves a little child among our roses.

We love, God makes: in our sweet mirth

God spies occasion for a birth.

Then is it His, or is it ours?

I know not—He is fond of flowers.

~ *Thomas Edward Brown*

▲

1. Copy the poem by hand.

2. Write what you notice about the poem.

3. Substitute another word for "love," so that you begin your poem with something like "when hate meets hate" or "when boy meets girl," etc. Write two short, four-line stanzas with the same rhyme scheme of *abab ccdd*. Try to create a similar sense of unresolvable paradox, ending the poem with an unanswerable question.

ON MY FIRST SON

Farewell, thou child of my right hand, and joy;
My sin was too much hope of thee, loved boy:
Seven years thou wert lent to me, and I thee pay,
Exacted by thy fate, on the just day.
O could I lose all father now! for why
Will man lament the state he should envy,
To have so soon 'scaped world's and flesh's rage,
And, if no other misery, yet age?
Rest in soft peace, and asked, say, "Here doth lie
Ben Jonson his best piece of poetry."
For whose sake henceforth all his vows be such
As what he loves may never like too much.

~ *Ben Jonson*

▲

1. Copy the poem by hand.

2. Notice Jonson's simple rhyme scheme—a series of six rhyming couplets in iambic pentameter.

3. Using the draft revision process, write your own six couplets of iambic pentameter. You might want to explore some personal loss of your own using this form.

Piano After War

On a snug evening I shall watch her fingers,
Cleverly ringed, declining to clever pink,
Beg glory from the willing keys. Old hungers
Will break their coffins, rise to eat and thank.
And music, warily, like the golden rose
That sometimes after sunset warms the west,
Will warm that room, persuasively suffuse
That room and me, rejuvenate a past.
But suddenly, across my climbing fever
Of proud delight—a multiplying cry.
A cry of bitter dead men who will never
Attend a gentle maker of musical joy.
Then my thawed eye will again to ice.
And stone will shove the softness from my face.

~ *Gwendolyn Brooks*

▲

1. Copy the poem by hand.

2. This poem's *ababcdcdefefgg* rhyme scheme uses slant rhymes. Ask yourself if you think the rhyming couplet at the end helps bring a sense of closure to the poem.

3. Using the draft revision process, write a poem using a similiar scheme of slanted rhymes.

ALLEGRO

After a black day, I play Haydn,
and feel a little warmth in my hands.

The keys are ready. Kind hammers fall.
The sound is spirited, green, and full of silence.

The sound says that freedom exists
and someone pays no tax to Caesar.

I shove my hands into my haydnpockets
and act like a man who is calm about it all.

I raise my haydnflag. The signal is:
"We do not surrender. But want peace."

The music is a house of glass standing on a slope;
rocks are flying, rocks are rolling.

The rocks roll straight through the house
but every pane of glass is still whole.

∼ *Tomas Transtromer*
Translated by Robert Bly

▲

1. Copy the poem by hand.

2. *Allegro* is written using what we call visual couplets. The lines are said to be 'couplets' because they are placed as such on the page, two at a time. Sound and imagery are also used with great subtlety, but it is the placement of the lines that delivers the unmistakable effect.

3. Using the draft revision process, write a poem using this kind of spatially-rendered couplets. Do not use rhymes.

TRAVELLING THROUGH DARK

Traveling through the dark I found a deer
dead on the edge of the Wilson River road.
It is usually best to roll them into the canyon:
that road is narrow; to swerve might make more dead.

By glow of tail-light I stumbled back of the car
and stood by the heap, a doe, a recent killing;
she had stiffened already, almost cold.
I dragged her off; she was large in the belly.

My fingers touching her side brought me the reason—
her side was warm; her fawn lay there waiting,
alive, still, never to be born.
Beside that mountain road I hesitated.

The car aimed ahead its lowered parking lights;
under the hood purred the steady engine.
I stood in the glare of the warm exhaust turning red;
around our group I could hear the wilderness listen.

I thought hard for us all—my only swerving—,
then pushed her over the edge into the river.

～ *William Stafford*

▲

1. Copy the poem by hand.

2. Although this poem does not have a clear rhyme scheme, if you look at the poem's arrangement on the page and listen to the assonance and consonance among the words ending each line, you can't help but feel a submerged structure, like the two-by-fours in the walls of an old house.

3. Using the draft revision process, write a poem with four-line stanzas and a final couplet. Avoid any true or slant rhymes, but do use occasional assonance or consonance among the end words.

THE SOLITARY REAPER

Behold her, single in the field,
Yon solitary Highland Lass!
Reaping and singing by herself;
Stop here, or gently pass!
Alone she cuts and binds the grain,
And sings a melancholy strain;
O listen! for the Vale profound
Is overflowing with the sound.

No Nightingale did ever chant
More welcome notes to weary bands
Of travellers in some shady haunt,
Among Arabian sands;
A voicer so thrilling ne'er heard
In spring time from the Cuckoobird,
Breaking the silence of the seas
Among the farthest Hebrides.

Will no one tell me what she sings?—
Perhaps the plaintive numbers flow
For old, unhappy, far-off things,
And battles long ago,
Or is it some more humble lay,
Familiar matter of to-day?
Some natural sorrow, loss, or pain,
That has been, and may be again!

Whate'er the theme, the maiden sang
As if her song could have no ending;
I saw her singing at her work,
And o'er the sickle bending;
I listened—motionless and still;
And as I mounted up the hill,
The music in my heart I bore,
Long after it was heard no more.

~ *William Wordsworth*

▲

1. Copy the poem by hand.

2. Write what you notice about the poem. Mark the poem for meter and rhyme scheme. Where do you see breaks in the pattern?

3. Try writing a poem in eight-line stanzas with a rhyme scheme of *ababc-cdd efefgghh,* one which tells the story of one remarkable moment from your past.

MOWING

There was never a sound beside the wood but
    one,
And that was my long scythe whispering to
    the ground.
What was it it whispered? I knew not well
    myself;
Perhaps it was something about the heat of
    the sun,
Something, perhaps, about the lack of sound—
And that was why it whispered and did not
    speak.
It was no dream of the gift of idle hours,
Or easy gold at the hand of fay or elf:
Anything more than the truth would have
    seemed too weak
To the earnest love that laid the swale in
    rows,
Not without feeble-pointed spikes of flowers
(Pale orchises), and scared a bright green
    snake.
The fact is the sweetest dream that labor
    knows.
My long scythe whispered and left the hay to
    make.

~ *Robert Frost*

◀ 1. Copy the poem by hand.

2. Look at this poem on the page or listen to it read aloud. It seems to be structured, yet it adheres to neither meter nor rhyme scheme. Listen carefully to the sounds that the poem makes. Mark the rhyme scheme in the margin to the right, making note of what, if any, structure the poem has.

3. Write a poem of your own which echoes the sounds of *Mowing*.

CHAPTER SEVEN:

Imagery Prompts

IN A STATION OF THE METRO

The apparition of these faces in the crowd;
Petals on a wet, black bough.

~ *Ezra Pound*

▲

1. Copy the poem by hand.

2. Write what you notice about the poem. What does the poem make you see?

3. Using the draft revision process, write a poem which has two direct and pointed lines: the first an image from an urban setting, the second from a setting in nature. Make each line a sharp, precise image.

———

LOVERS IN WINTER

The posture of the tree
    Shows the prevailing wind;
And ours, long misery
    When you are long unkind.

But forward, look, we lean—
    Not backward as in doubt—
And still with branches green
    Ride our ill weather out.

  ~ *Robert Graves*

▲

1. Copy the poem by hand.

2. Write what you notice about the poem. The central image is of a tree leaning in the wind. How does the fact that the tree leans forward, as opposed to backward, affect your feeling about the image of the tree?

3. Write a short poem of your own in which you use a single, carefully chosen image in order to show some difficulty you have with someone you love.

WINTER POEM

once a snowflake fell
on my brow and i loved
it so much and i kissed
it and it was happy and called its cousins
and brothers and a web
of snow engulfed me then
i reached to love them all
and i squeezed them and became
a spring rain and i stood perfectly
still and was a flower

~ *Nikki Giovanni*

▲

1. Copy the poem by hand.

2. Giovanni's poem has no end-rhymes, no metrical regularity, no stanzas or other formal patterns, and no punctuation. Yet the poem still conveys a clear, crystalline image of transformation.

3. Using the draft revision process, write a poem which echoes *Winter Poem*. Avoid formal structures or stylistic conventions. Focus on the image that your poem conveys. How does your poem lead the reader to see the picture that you have in mind?

Spring Images

Two athletes
Are dancing in the cathedral
Of the wind.

A butterfly lights on the branch
Of your green voice.

Small antelopes
Fall asleep in the ashes
Of the moon.

~ *James Wright*

1. Copy the poem by hand.

2. Write what you notice about the poem. The poem is clearly divided into three parts by syntax and graphic space. How are the three images different? How are they the same?

3. Using the draft revision process, write a poem which uses three highly suggestive images. Echo the structure of *Spring Images* as much or as little as you need to.

FORK

This strange thing must have crept
Right out of hell.
It resembles a bird's foot
Worn round the cannibal's neck.

As you hold it in your hand,
As you stab with it into a piece of meat,
It is possible to imagine the rest of the bird;
Its head which like your fist
Is large, bald, beakless and blind.

~ *Charles Simic*

▲

1. Copy the poem by hand.

2. Write what you notice about the poem.

3. Using the draft revision process, write a poem of your own which portrays an ordinary object from a radically different point of view. Echo Simic's bold use of concrete imagery; try also to capture the ironic comedy.

I WAS AFRAID OF DYING

Once,

I was afraid of dying

In a field of dry weeds

But now,

All day long I have been walking among damp fields,

Trying to keep still, listening

To insects that move patiently.

Perhaps they are sampling the fresh dew that gathers slowly

In empty snail shells

And in the secret shelters of sparrow feathers fallen on the

earth.

~ *James Wright*

▲

1. Copy the poem by hand.

2. What do you notice about this poem? It always makes me feel very small, as though I were in a very private and quiet place; like the dried husk of an old snail shell watching dew gather.

3. Using the draft revision process, write a poem which examines an intimate and close place—one which is very specific and concrete in its appearance, yet very small.

FIDELITY

an excerpt

Fidelity and love are two different things, like a flower and a
  gem.
And love, like a flower, will fade, will change into something
  else
or it would not be flowery.

O flowers they fade because they are moving swiftly; a little
  torrent of life
leaps up to the summit of the stem, gleams, turns over round
  the bend
of the parabola of curved flight,
sinks, and is gone, like a comet curving into the invisible.

O flowers they are all the time travelling
like comets, and they come into our ken
for a day, for two days, and withdraw, slowly vanish again.

And we, we must take them on the wing, and let them go....

∽ *D.H. Lawrence*

▲

1. Copy the poem by hand.

2. Write what you notice about the poem.

3. Using the draft revision process, write a poem which echoes Law-
rence's pattern of imagery, especially the way he weaves into and out of
concreteness.

To Waken An Old Lady

Old age is
a flight of small
cheeping birds
skimming
bare trees
above a snow glaze.
Gaining and failing
they are buffeted
by a dark wind—
But what?
On harsh weedstalks
the flock has rested,
the snow
is covered with broken
seedhusks
and by the wind tempered
by a shrill
piping of plenty.

~ *William Carlos Williams*

▲

1. Copy the poem by hand.

2. Notice that once the metaphor is stated in the first three lines, Williams stays with this image to the end.

3. Using the draft revision process, write a poem in which you state a similiar metaphor (e.g., "infancy is a box of puppies" or "illness is an old dog that won't die," etc.), then develop the imagery using the short tentative phrasing characteristic of *To Waken An Old Lady*.

THE LAST LEAF

I saw him once before,
As he passed by the door,
    And again
The pavement stones resound,
As he totters o'er the ground
    With his cane.

They say that in his prime,
Ere the pruning-knife of Time
    Cut him down,
Not a better man was found
By the Crier on his round
    Through the town.

But now he walks the streets,
And he looks at all he meets
    Sad and wan,
And he shakes his feeble head,
That it seems as if he said,
    "They are gone."

The mossy marbles rest
On the lips that he has pressed
    In their bloom,
And the names he loved to hear
Have been carved for many a year
    On the tomb.

My Grandmamma has said—
Poor old lady, she is dead
    Long ago—
That he had a Roman nose,
And his cheek was like a rose
    In the snow.

But now his nose is thin,
And it rests upon his chin
    Like a staff,
And a crook is in his back,
And a melancholy crack
    In his laugh.

I know it is a sin
For me to sit and grin
    At him here;
But the old three-cornered hat,
And the breeches, and all that,
    Are so queer!

And if I should live to be
The last leaf upon the tree
    In the spring,
Let them smile, as I do now,
At the old forsaken bough
    Where I cling.

∼ *Oliver Wendell Holmes*

▲

1. Copy the poem by hand.

2. Note the main image in each of the eight stanzas. Notice how while many of the details in *The Last Leaf* do not describe the old gentleman directly, we are still able to visualize him.

3. Think of someone out of the ordinary you either know or have seen, and then write a poem which describes the places or images which are visually suggestive of that person.

SAILING TO BYZANTIUM
an excerpt

An aged man is but a paltry thing,
A tattered coat upon a stick, unless
Soul clap its hands and sing, and louder sing
For every tatter in its mortal dress,
Nor is there singing school but studying
Monuments of its own magnificence;
And therefore I have sailed the seas and come
To the holy city of Byzantium.

~ *W. B. Yeats*

1. Copy the poem by hand.

2. Notice that the main image in the poem is "a tattered coat on a stick." What other imagery does Yeats use to counterbalance this less than flattering picture of man?

3. Using the draft revision process, write a poem in which you explore the idea of your own mortality using imagery.

THE HOLLOW MEN
an excerpt

We are the hollow men
We are the stuffed men
Leaning together
Headpiece filled with straw. Alas!
Our dried voices, when
We whisper together
Are quiet and meaningless
As wind in dry grass
Or rats' feet over broken glass
In our dry cellar

    Shape without form, shade without colour,
Paralysed force, gesture without motion;

Those who have crossed
With direct eyes, to death's other Kingdom
Remember us—if at all—not as lost
Violent souls, but only
As the hollow men
The stuffed men.

~ *T.S. Eliot*

▲

1. Copy the poem by hand.

2. Notice how Eliot uses the image of hollowness to represent men without a soul.

3. Using the draft revision process, write a poem using specific imagery to convey some idea about people.

ORPHEUS 7

I play, there is no answer.
The sea darkens.
On the branch, bronze leaves
quivering stiffen.
Moon, stars, order themselves in silence,
there is no motion.
I wander,
firm frail instrument of marrow and bone.

Reversed,
the landscape.
To a hollow mirror
I play the expanse of space inverted,
for the sake of the opposed harmonies,
slow narrowing music,
the vanishing, the not heard.

~ *Eeva-Liisa Manner*

**translated from the Finnish
by Babette Deutsch**

▲

1. Copy the poem by hand.

2. Trace the path of the imagery through the poem. Notice the dream-like quality achieved by overlapping and intertwining the languages of music, movement, spatial relationships, and nature.

3. Using the draft revision process, write a poem which echoes Deutsch's use of mixed imagery in *Orpheus 7*.

CHAPTER EIGHT:

Structure Prompts

YOUTH AND AGE

Much did I rage when young,
Being by the world oppressed,
But now with flattering tongue
It speeds the parting guest.

∼ *W.B. Yeats*

▲

1. Copy the poem by hand.

2. This is a four-line poem of iambic trimeter, with an *abab* rhyme scheme. While the poem has true sound rhymes and masculine rhymes, it does not have sight rhymes. (Notice, too, how "I" becomes "it.")

3. Using the draft revision process, write a poem which echoes the structure of *Youth and Age* as closely as possible.

Requiem

Under the wide and starry sky,
Dig the grave and let me lie.
Glad did I live and gladly die,
  And laid me down with a will.

This be the verse you grave for me:
Here he lies where he longed to be;
Home is the sailor, home from sea,
  And the hunter home from the hill.

  ~ *R.L. Stevenson*

▲

1. Copy the poem by hand.

2. This poem of two short stanzas has the following rhyme scheme: *aaab cccb.*

3. Using the draft revision process, write a poem to have placed on your tomb—one which echoes the structure of *Requiem*.

BREAKFAST

We ate breakfast lying on our backs
Because the shells were screeching overhead.
I bet a rasher to a loaf of bread
That Hull United would beat Halifax
When Jimmy Stainthorpe played full-back instead
of Billy Bradford. Ginger raised his head
And cursed, and took the bet; and dropped back dead.
We ate our breakfast lying on our backs,
Because the shells were screeching overhead.

~ *Wilfred Gibson*

1. Copy the poem by hand.

2. The structural device used so effectively in this poem is the simple repetition of the first two lines at the end of the poem. It is also interesting to note that, in a poem of nine lines, there are only two end-rhymes: the sound in "dead" and the sound of "ax."

3. Using the draft revision process, write a poem of about the same length (rhyming is optional) repeating the first two lines in the last two lines of your poem, as Gibson does.

A LITTLE POEM

We say that some are mad. In fact
if we have all the words and we
make madness mean the way they act
then they as all of us can see

are surely mad. And then again
if they have all the words and call
madness something else, well then—
well then, they are not mad at all.

∼ *Miller Williams*

▲

1. Copy the poem by hand.

2. Williams uses a straight-forward *abab cdcd* rhyme scheme, but he uses enjambment (one line running-on into the next line) to create an elastic feeling in his poem. The use of so many monosyllables helps give structure to his poem, while allowing it some give.

3. Using the draft revision process, write a poem which echoes Williams's combination of rhyme scheme and heavy enjambment.

EIGHT O'CLOCK

He stood, and heard the steeple
  Sprinkle the quarters on the morning town.
One, two, three, four, to market-place and people
  It tossed them down.

Strapped, noosed, nighing his hour,
  He stood and counted them and cursed his luck;
And then the clock collected in the tower
  Its strength, and struck.

~ *A. E. Housman*

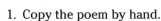

▲

1. Copy the poem by hand.

2. Like *A Little Poem*, *Eight O'Clock* has a rhyme scheme of *abab cdcd*. However, notice how differently Housman's poem is structured. It avoids enjambment and has a metrical structure that alternates between iambs and spondees.

3. Using the draft revision process, write a poem which is structured like Housman's and which echoes the halting, spondaic quality of his metrical structure.

DON JUAN
an excerpt

"I loved you, I love you, for this love have lost
  State, station, heaven, mankind's, my own esteem,
And yet cannot regret what it hath cost,
  So dear is still the memory of that dream;
Yet, if I name my guilt, 'tis not to boast,
  None can deem harshlier of me than I deem:
I trace this scrawl because I cannot rest—
I've nothing to reproach or to request.

"Man's love is of man's life a thing apart,
  'Tis woman's whole existence; man may range
The court, camp, church, the vessel, and the mart;
  Sword, gown, gain, glory, offer in exchange
Pride, fame, ambition, to fill up his heart,
  And few there are whom these cannot estrange;
Men have all these resources, we but one,
To love again, and be again undone.

~ *Lord Byron*

▲

1. Copy the poem by hand.

2. This exemplifies the great tragi-comic stanza, the ottava rima, perfected by Byron in his mock-epic, *Don Juan*. The rhyme scheme is *abababcc ded-edeff ghghghii*....

3. Using the draft revision process, write a letter to someone, preferably a long-lost or excruciatingly unattainable lover, using two stanzas of *ottava rima*.

IV

when citied day with the sonorous homes
of light swiftly sink in the sorrowful hour,
they counted petals O tremendous flower
on whose huge heart prospecting darkness roams

torture my spirit with the exquisite forms
and whithers of existence,
          as by shores
soundless, the unspeaking watcher who adores

perceived sails whose mighty brightness dumbs

the utterance of his soul—so even i
wholly chained to a grave astonishment
feel in my being the delirious smart

of thrilled ecstasy, where sea and sky
marry—

    to know the white ship of thy heart

on frailer ports of costlier commerce bent

∾ *e.e. cummings*

▲

1. Copy the poem by hand.

2. cummings uses a traditional sonnet rhyme scheme—*abbacddc efgegf*—but stretches and pulls it graphically as is his style.

3. Using the draft revision process, write a loose-jointed sonnet which adheres to the traditional rhyme scheme.

MEN MARRY WHAT THEY NEED. I MARRY YOU

Men marry what they need. I marry you,
morning by morning, day by day, night by night,
and every marriage makes this marriage new.

In the broken name of heaven, in the light
that shatters granite, by the spitting shore,
in air that leaps and wobbles like a kite,

I marry you from time and a great door
is shut and stays shut against wind, sea, stone,
sunburst, and heavenfall. And home once more

inside our walls of skin and struts of bone,
man-woman, woman-man, and each other,
I marry you by all dark and all dawn

and learn to let time spend. Why should I bother
the flies about me? Let them buzz and do.
Men marry their queen, their daughter, or their mother

by names they prove, but that thin buzz whines through:
when reason falls to reasons, cause is true.
Men marry what they need. I marry you.

∽ *John Ciardi*

▲

1. Copy the poem by hand.

2. Write what you notice about the poem, being sure to mark the rhyme
scheme. Why do you think Ciardi would choose a structure like this for a
poem about marriage?

3. Using the draft revision process, write a poem of three line stanzas in
which the rhyme scheme is interlocks: *aba bcb cdc....*

THE CASTLE OF THORNS

Through autumn evening, water whirls thin blue,
From iron to iron pail—old, lined, and pure;
Beneath, the iron is indistinct, secure
In revery that cannot reach to you.
Water it was that always lay between
The mind of man and that harsh wall of thorn,
Of stone impenetrable, where the horn
Hung like the key to what it all might mean.

My goats step guardedly, with delicate
Hard flanks and forest hair, unchanged and firm,
A strong tradition that has not grown old.
Peace to the lips that bend in intricate
Old motions, that flinch not before their term!
Peace to the heart that can accept this cold!

∼ *Yvor Winters*

▲

1. Copy the poem by hand.

2. This is another poem written in Sonnet form, whose rhyme scheme is *abbacddc efgefg.*

3. Using the draft revision process, write an Italian Sonnet, like Winters', and attempt to maintain a tight metrical arrangement. Try also to echo the metrical regularity of *The Castle of Thorns.*

Sonnet II

The world is too much with us; late and soon,
Getting and spending, we lay waste our powers:
Little we see in nature that is ours;
We have given our hearts away, a sordid boon!
This sea that bears her bosom to the moon;
The winds that will be howling at all hours,
And are up-gathered now like sleeping flowers;
For this, for everything, we are out of tune;
It moves us not.—Great God! I'd rather be
A pagan suckled in a creed outworn;
So might I, standing on a pleasant lea,
Have glimpses that would make me less forlorn:
Have sight of Proteus rising from the sea;
Or hear old Triton blow his wreathed horn.

~ *William Wordsworth*

▲

1. Copy the poem by hand.

2. Mark both the rhyme scheme and meter of the poem.

3. Using the draft revision process, write a poem of your own which echoes Wordworth's structure.

CHAPTER NINE:

Meaning Prompts

NOTE
straw, feathers, dust—
little things

but if they all go the same way,
that's the way the wind goes.

~ *William Stafford*

▲

1. Copy the poem by hand.

2 Notice how the poem leads you into expectation by way of: the list, the restatement of what's on the list, then the "but" and the "if," driving you towards the poem's logical end.

3. Talk back to this poem by echoing its logic and rhetorical structure.

A Major Work

Poems are hard to read
Pictures are hard to see
Music is hard to hear
And people are hard to love

But whether from brute need
Or divine energy
At last mind eye and ear
And the great sloth heart will move.

∿ *William Meredith*

▲

1. Copy the poem by hand.

2. Write what you notice about the poem. (See p. 41–2.)

3. Using the draft revision process, write a poem which has two short stanzas, and where the second of which has as its first word, "but."

WHEN I HAVE FEARS

When I have fears that I may cease to be
 Before my pen has gleaned my teeming brain,
Before high-piléd books, in charact'ry,
 Hold like rich garners the full-ripened grain;
When I behold, upon the night's starred face,
 Huge cloudy symbols of a high romance,
And think that I may never live to trace
 Their shadows, with the magic hand of chance;
And when I feel, fair creature of an hour,
 That I shall never look upon thee more,
Never have relish in the faery power
 Of unreflecting love!—then on the shore
Of the wide world I stand alone, and think
Till Love and Fame to nothingness do sink.

~ *John Keats*

▲

1. Copy the poem by hand.

2. When Keats imagines his death, he also imagines longing for the precious things he will not live to see—he sees how death levels every accomplishment and every pleasure. What makes the poem figurative is the way in which he turns the things he will miss—all abstractions like "learning," "fame," or "love"—into concrete forms. In the process, he also conveys a sense of relationship to these abstractions.

3. Using the draft revision process, write a poem about what you might miss if you died too soon, and talk about these abstractions using concrete forms.

LITTLE EXERCISE
for Thomas Edwards Wanning

Think of the storm roaming the sky uneasily
like a dog looking for a place to sleep in,
listen to it growling.

Think how they must look now, the mangrove keys
lying out there unresponsive to the lightning
in dark, coarse-fibred families,

where occasionally a heron may undo his head,
shake up his feathers, make an uncertain comment
when the surrounding water shines.

Think of the boulevard and the little palm trees
all stuck in rows, suddenly revealed
as fistfuls of limp fish-skeletons.

It is raining there. The boulevard
and its broken sidewalks with weeds in every crack
are relieved to be wet, the sea to be freshened.

Now the storm goes away again in a series
of small, badly lit battle-scenes,
each in "Another part of the field."

Think of someone sleeping in the bottom of a row-boat
tied to a mangrove root or the pile of a bridge;
think of him as uninjured, barely disturbed.

~ *Elizabeth Bishop*

A COAT

I made my song a coat
Covered with embroideries
Out of old mythologies
From heel to throat;
But the fools caught it,
Wore it in the world's eyes
As though they'd wrought it.
Song, let them take it,
For there's more enterprise
In walking naked.

~ *W.B. Yeats*

▲

1. Copy the poem by hand.

2. Write what you notice about the poem.

3. Replace Yeat's figure of the coat with an object of your own: a car, a hat, a suitcase, etc. Then use this figure as an object of meaning, echoing the way Keats lets his meaning unfold.

◀ 1. Copy the poem by hand.

2. Write what you notice about the poem.

3. Using the draft revision process, write a poem using the rhetorical device, "think of…" both as a repeated beginning of each new sentence and as a way to organize your expression of a deeply held emotion.

AUTOBIOGRAPHIA LITERARIA

When I was a child
I played by myself in a
corner of the schoolyard
all alone.

I hated dolls and I
hated games, animals were
not friendly and birds
flew away.

If anyone was looking
for me I hid behind a
tree and cried out "I am
an orphan."

And here I am, the
center of all beauty!
writing these poems!
Imagine!

~ *Frank O'Hara*

▲

1. Copy the poem by hand.

2. I always understand this to be an ironic poem, where its naive tone stands in sharp contrast to the much more worldly poet. How do I know he is worldly? Because he is openly mimicking poems like the one by Keats (pg. 85), in which the poet takes himself seriously. I also notice that, despite the childlike diction, O'Hara constructs a subtle pattern of sound which you can hear, especially in the last line of each stanza: "all alone," "flew away," "an orphan," and "imagine."

3. Using the draft revision process, write a poem in which you mirror O'Hara's unique building block stanzas with the monometer last line.

THE HARBOUR

The fishermen rowing homeward in the dusk
Do not consider the stillness through which they move,
So I, since feelings drown, should no more ask
For the safe twilight which your calm hands gave.
And the night, urger of old lies,
Winked at by stars that sentry the humped hills,
Should hear no secret faring-forth; time knows
That bitter and sly sea, and love raises walls.
Yet others who now watch my progress outward,
On a sea which is crueller than any word
Of love, may see in me the calm my passage makes,
Braving new water in an antique hoax;
And the secure from thinking may climb safe to liners
Hearing small rumours of paddlers drowned near stars.

~ *Derek Walcott*

▲

1. Copy the poem by hand.

2. Notice how Walcott uses the harbour, the open sea, and the small boat to build the meaning of his poem: namely, that he would rather be in love than be safe (see p. 39).

3. Using the draft revision process, write a poem which echoes *The Harbour* in its use of a figurative device.

CHAPTER TEN:

More Prompts

On Being Brought From Africa to America

'Twas mercy brought me from my *Pagan* land,
Taught my benighted soul to understand
That there's a God, that there's a *Saviour* too:
Once I redemption neither sought nor knew.
Some view our sable race with scornful eye,
"Their colour is a diabolic die."
Remember, *Christians*, *Negroes*, black as *Cain*,
May be refin'd, and join th' angelic train.

∼ *Phillis Wheatley*

1. Copy the poem by hand.

2. Write what you notice about the poem.

3. Using the draft revision process, write a poem of your own which echoes the original poem in some noticeable way.

PREFACE TO A TWENTY-VOLUME SUICIDE NOTE
For Kellie Jones, born 16 May 1959

Lately, I've become accustomed to the way
The ground opens up and envelopes me
Each time I go out to walk the dog.
Or the broad edged silly music the wind
Makes when I run for a bus...

Things have come to that.

And now, each night I count the stars,
And each night I get the same number.
And when they will not come to be counted,
I count the holes they leave.

Nobody *sings* anymore.

And then last night, I tiptoed up
To my daughter's room and heard her
Talking to someone, and when I opened
The door, there was no one there...
Only she on her knees, peeking into

Her own clasped hands.

∽ *Imamu Amiri Baraka*

▲

1. Copy the poem by hand.

2. Write what you notice about the poem.

3. Using the draft revision process, write a poem of your own which echoes the original poem in some noticeable way.

A DISH OF PEACHES IN RUSSIA

With my whole body I taste these peaches,
I touch them and smell them. Who speaks?

I absorb them as the Angevine
Absorbs Anjou. I see them as a lover sees,

As a young lover sees the first buds of spring
And as the black Spaniard plays his guitar.

Who speaks? But it must be that I,
That animal, that Russian, that exile, for whom

The bells of the chapel pullulate sounds at
Heart. The peaches are large and round,

Ah! and red; and they have peach fuzz, ah!
They are full of juice and the skin is soft.

They are full of the colors of my village
And of fair weather, summer, dew, peace.

The room is quiet where they are.
The windows are open. The sunlight fills

The curtains. Even the drifting of the curtains,
Slight as it is, disturbs me. I did not know

That such ferocities could tear
One self from another, as these peaches do.

∼ *Wallace Stevens*

AFTER GREAT PAIN

After great pain, a formal feeling comes—
The Nerves sit ceremonious, like Tombs—
The stiff Heart questions, was it He, that bore,
And Yesterday, or Centuries before?

The Feet, mechanical, go round—
Of Ground, or Air, or Ought—
A Wooden way
Regardless grown,
A Quartz contentment, like a stone.

This is the Hour of Lead—
Remembered, if outlived,
As Freezing persons, recollect the Snow—
First—Chill—then Stupor—then the letting go—

~ *Emily Dickinson*

▲

1. Copy the poem by hand.

2. Write what you notice about the poem.

3. Using the draft revision process, write a poem of your own which echoes the original poem in some noticeable way.

◀ 1. Copy the poem by hand.

2. Write what you notice about the poem.

3. Using the draft revision process, write a poem of your own which echoes the original poem in some noticeable way.

AT THE BALL GAME

The crowd at the ball game
is moved uniformly

by a spirit of uselessness
which delights them—

all the exciting detail
of the chase

and the escape, the error
the flash of genius—

all to no end save beauty
the eternal—

So in detail they, the crowd,
are beautiful

for this
to be warned against

saluted and defied—
It is alive, venomous

it smiles grimly
its words cut—

The flashy female with her
mother, gets it—

The Jew gets it straight—it
is deadly, terrifying—

It is the Inquisition, the
Revolution

It is beauty itself
that lives

day by day in them
idly—

This is
the power of their faces

It is summer, it is the solstice
the crowd is

cheering, the crowd is laughing
in detail

permanently, seriously
without thought

~ *William Carlos Williams*

▲

1. Copy the poem by hand.

2. Write what you notice about the poem.

3. Using the draft revision process, write a poem of your own which echoes the original poem in some noticeable way.

Further Instructions

Come, my songs, let us express our baser pas-
        sions,
    Let us express our envy of the man with a
  steady job and no worry about the future.
You are very idle, my songs.
I fear you will come to a bad end.
You stand about in the streets,
You loiter at the corners and bus-stops,
You do next to nothing at all.

You do not even express our inner nobilities,
You will come to a very bad end.

And I?
I have gone half cracked,
I have talked to you so much that
             I almost see you about me,
Insolent little beasts, shameless, devoid of clothing!

But you, newest of song of the lot,
You are not old enough to have done much mischief,
I will get you a green coat out of China
With dragons worked upon it,
I will get you the scarlet silk trousers
From the statue of the infant Christ in Santa Maria
    Novella,
Lest they say we are lacking in taste,
Or that there is no caste in this family.

∼ *Ezra Pound*

THE COLD ROOM

The dream
stands
in the night
above unpainted
floor and chair.

The dog is
dead asleep
and
will not move
for god or fire.

And from the
ceiling
darkness bends
a heavy flame.

~ *Yvor Winters*

▲

1. Copy the poem by hand.

2. Write what you notice about the poem.

3. Using the draft revision process, write a poem of your own which echoes the original poem in some noticeable way.

◀ 1. Copy the poem by hand.

2. Write what you notice about the poem.

3. Using the draft revision process, write a poem of your own which echoes the original poem in some noticeable way.

Theme for English B

The instructor said,

> *Go home and write*
> *a page tonight.*
> *And let that page come out of you—*
> *Then, it will be true.*

I wonder if it's that simple?
I am twenty-two, colored, born in Winston-Salem.
I went to school there, then Durham, then here
to this college on the hill above Harlem.
I am the only colored student in my class.
The steps from the hill lead down into Harlem,
through a park, then I cross St. Nicholas,
Eighth Avenue, Seventh, and I come to the Y,
the Harlem Branch Y, where I take the elevator
up to my room, sit down, and write this page:

It's not easy to know what is true for you or me
at twenty-two, my age. But I guess I'm what
I feel and see and hear, Harlem, I hear you:
hear you, hear me—we two—you, me, talk on this page.
(I hear New York, too.) Me—who?
Well, I like to eat, sleep, drink, and be in love.
I like to work, read, learn, and understand life.
I like a pipe for a Christmas present,
or records—Bessie, bop, or Bach.
I guess being colored doesn't make me *not* like
the same things other folks like who are other races.
So will my page be colored that I write?

Being me, it will not be white.
But it will be
a part of you, instructor.
You are white—
yet a part of me, as I am a part of you.
That's American.
Sometimes perhaps you don't want to be part of me.
Nor do I often want to be a part of you.
But we are, that's true!
As I learn from you,
I guess you learn from me—
although you're older—and white—
and somewhat more free.

This is my page for English B.

∿ *Langston Hughes*

▲

1. Copy the poem by hand.

2. Write what you notice about the poem.

3. Using the draft revision process, write a poem of your own which echoes the original poem in some noticeable way.

THE BEETLE
for my father

When I go to the bathroom I see a beetle in the tub,
black, with a band of stone color
around the center, granite with a trace of
lichen on it, luminous on a damp day,
and I wonder if it's a death-watch beetle,
and I think of your death,
I wonder if the cancer will take
a long time or a short time
and I wonder if death-watch beetles are the beetles
that eat the dead. I think of you buried,
I think of the beetles that will eat your body, I would like
   to be one of them.
After you die, in my sleep I would like to
turn into one of the beetles and
eat my way through you all night
in calm beetle life. I want to
have whatever I can of you,
I want to eat those years of darkness and silence,
to taste your life, to eat the head
you turned away.
I even want to eat the cancer,
work my way slowly through the greyish

slightly hot mass, to know you.

Your eye, tongue, if you have no more use for your body

I have always wanted it,

I never liked the way the other god's body

dissolved on the tongue, now I come with my

strong dark jaws—your life in my

body is my life, I want to use it with

real physical rage and physical love.

∼ *Sharon Olds*

▲

1. Copy the poem by hand.

2. Write what you notice about the poem.

3. Using the draft revision process, write a poem of your own which echoes the original poem in some noticeable way.

POETRY

The only way to be quiet
is to be quick, so I scare
you clumsily, or surprise
you with a stab. A praying
mantis knows time more
intimately than I and is
more casual. Crickets use
time for accompaniment to
innocent fidgeting. A zebra
races counterclockwise.
All this I desire. To
deepen you by my quickness
and delight as if you
were logical and proven,
but still be quiet as if
I were used to you; as if
you would never leave me
and were the inexorable
product of my own time.

～ *Frank O'Hara*

▲

1. Copy the poem by hand.

2. Write what you notice about the poem.

3. Using the draft revision process, write a poem of your own which echoes the original poem in some noticeable way.

ROOTER

Played ball yourself once, mister?
Once, yes. No talker mister.
Picks up no stray balls, makes no remark,
Sticks around till dark.

Cold afternoons with the sun fading
Yardline the street with the trees' shading.
On fields so hard the scores run
Higher and hotter than the sun.

Audience watches hit the bat,
In an overcoat and a gray hat,
Deep his hands in his pockets, tense;
Stilled by the shouting, the audience.

The tree where he leaned not warm to touch,
The grass not trodden very much,
The curd where he stood as cold as stone
In the dark, when he is gone.

~ *Josephine Miles*

▲

1. Copy the poem by hand.

2. Write what you notice about the poem.

3. Using the draft revision process, write a poem of your own which echoes the original poem in some noticeable way.

Glossary

Alliteration means repetition of sound within a line, a stanza, or a poem. Most alliteration is accomplished with the consonants and is called *consonance*, as in, "the groundhog grazed on the green grass," where there is a repetition of the "gr" sound. Repetition of vowel sounds is called *assonance*, as in, "a loud crowd of cows."

Analogy is a relationship between two pairs of things. If I give you a newspaper clipping which, to my mind, vindicates everything I have been saying to you for the previous three years, and if I then say to you, as I hand you the clipping, "put this in your pipe and smoke it," I am using analogy. I am saying that "the newsprint will do to your pipe what the article will do to your opinion," that is, the first will send the second up in smoke. When you use an analogy in this way, the reader must know how the first thing relates to the second thing in just the way that the third thing relates to the fourth thing. This may be why, although it can be used to clarify a thought, analogy is not frequently used by most writers.

Apposition is a rhetorical tool. It means putting words, things, ideas in a side-by-side, one-after-the-other relationship. It is in a sense the device of the list, especially the list within the sentence. As such, words, things, ideas are most commonly put into an appositional relationship by means of commas.

Conceit is an Elizabethan notion of an elaborately developed metaphor, working like a trestle of meaning on which to hang the poetic foliage. A poem creates tension by pushing a central image or idea to an extreme. By holding fast to an image contained in the single, elaborately developed metaphor, a poem communicates persistence and intensity.

Couplets refer to pairs of rhymed lines. They are often used with iambic pentameter, as in these lines from the Prologue to Congreve's play, *The Way of the World:*

To please, this time, has been his sole pretense,
He'll not instruct, lest it should give offense.
Should he by chance a knave or fool expose,
That hurts none here; sure here are none of those.
In short, our play shall (with your leave to show it)
Give you one instance of a passive poet
Who to your judgements yields all resignation;
So save or damn after your own discretion.

Couplets also show up in much modern poetry in the form of spatial couplets, that is, two lines that are placed together so as to form a set of two—a "pair" of lines to the eye if not to the ear. Wallace Stevens, in *Phosphor Reading By His Own Light,* is only one example of a poet who employs spatial couplets in this way:

Look, realist, not knowing what you expect.
The green falls on you as you look,

Falls on and makes and gives, even a speech.
And you think that that is what you expect,

That elemental parent, the green night,
Teaching a fusky alphabet.

Enjambment refers to the occurence of a line of verse running over into the next line. Enjambment tends to call a reader's attention to the line structure. This is true whether the enjambment occurs in the context of a strictly metered and rhymed verse or of a more loose-jointed verse. Enjambment comes from the same root as "door jamb." Each line normally ends with a carefully balanced sound of closure, like a door closing; but when enjambment occurs, the rhythm is broken. For a traditional and masterful use of enjambment, see the excerpt from Shakepeare's *Tempest* below (in the entry for *Scansion*). Notice that of the nine lines, five end with either a comma or a period. Of the remaining four lines, two are softly enjambed and two are noticeably enjambed. As an instance of effective enjambment, it is worth listening closely to the line breaks in "dwell/ in this bare island by your spell" and "breath of yours my sails/Must fill, or else my project fails."

Irony is the use of language in which there is a noticeable contrast between the literal meaning, or content, and the more broadly suggested meaning, or context. For example, I could use my writer's voice to tell you that understanding the word "irony" is still a work-in-progress for me; but when you recognize that I am supposed to be explaining it here, the recognition might strike you as being *ironic*. Wilfred Gibson's poem, *Breakfast*, (pg. 75), is a good example of a poem which creates an ironic effect by its contrast between what is literally taking place (in this case it is breakfast in a war trench) and the incongruity of the larger context (a war in which the people you are eating breakfast with are dying).

Layout - see *Page Layout*

Metaphor is not so much a device or even a strategy of the poet as it is a method of construction. The main idea beneath the poem becomes its central metaphor, guiding every aspect of the poem, opening doors and windows of possibility.

Metrics
Terms for each line of verse as measured in metrical feet:
    monometer - a line of one foot
    dimeter - a line of two feet
    trimeter - a line of three feet
    tetrameter - a line of four feet
    pentameter - a line of five feet
    hexameter - a line of six feet
    heptameter - a line of seven feet
    octameter - a line of eight feet

Terms for the metrical feet as measured by dominant rhythm or beat:

    iamb - an unstressed syllable followed by a stressed one, as in:
    "begin," "intend," "the end"

    trochee - backwards iamb, as in:
    "turtle," "bitter," "brainy"

    dactyl - a stressed followed by an unstressed syllable, as in:
    "waterloo," "toiletries," "swimming pool"

anapest - backwards dactyl, as in:
"well, what would you do if your mother asked you?"

spondee - two demonstrative stresses back-to-back, as in:
"Come! Now!" "Wait! Stop!" "Yes! No!"

As an example of the usefulness of this vocabulary: you could describe a poem in which each line has five accented beats, and in which the rhythm of that beat is clearly an alteration between an accented and an unaccented syllable of sound; or you could describe it as a poem in *iambic pentameter.*

Onomatopœia is the use of words that sound like what they mean, as in, "tip-toe," "babbling brook," and "wide water, without sound." Onomatapœia is, in one sense, a figurative use of language, using raw sound to represent the quality of a thing.

Page Layout, besides simply meaning how the words are placed on the page, is a way of noticing the strategic use of literal organization — in other words, how the poem is arranged within the literal space of the blank page. When we speak of *spatial couplets, spatial stanzas,* and *spatially motivated designs* we call attention to a means of formal organization much employed by poets, especially modern poets who have sought to find alternatives to metrical forms of poetic structure.

Rhetorical logic is a device which the poet takes from the prose writer in order to create a specific effect. For example, in the following passage from *Why I Am Not A Painter,* by Frank O'Hara, notice how many words are devoted to the forward motion of the sentences:

> ...<u>One day</u> I am thinking of
> a color: orange. I write a line
> about orange. <u>Pretty soon</u> it is a
> whole page of words, not lines.
> <u>Then</u> another page. <u>There should be</u>
> so much more, not of orange, of
> words, of how terrible orange is
> and life.
>
> ⁓ *Frank O'Hara*

In addition to the sense of movement created by the underlined words, notice the repeated use of the "not this, but that" construction: "...a whole page of words, not lines..." and "...not of orange, of words, of how terrible orange is...." Rhetorical constructions of this kind create an expectation in the reader which is triggered by words like "but." If you look at William Stafford's poem *Note,* for example, on page 83, you notice that it is a list followed by a "but," which is a form of rhetorical logic. It is, in other words, tied to the underlying structure of conventional language.

Rhyme
Masculine Rhyme, Feminine Rhyme
Masculine rhymes end a line loudly and clearly: "Anytime I wish to dance/ I have to wait for my big chance." There's no mistaking masculine rhymes, ending as they do with an accented syllable. Feminine rhymes, on the other hand, end in an unaccented syallable, and they have a different impact on the ear. *The Faith,* by Josephine Miles (pg. 50) is a good example of feminine rhymes which are used to powerful effect.

Sound Rhyme, Sight Rhyme
This is a distinction between the way a word sounds and the way it is spelled. "Knot" and "caught" are sound rhymes because their sounds are identical; "orange" and "arrange" are sight rhymes because they are only spelled the same.

True Rhyme, Slant Rhyme
True rhymes are the "clear blue sky, tears in my eye" sorts of rhymes. True rhymes can also be feminine, as in "fallow" and "shallow." Slant rhymes differ from true rhymes in that they are not the same sound repeated, they are a variation of the sound, a subtle echo. Slant rhymes include such possibilities as "fingers" and "hungers," "pink" and "thank," rhymes in which only the final vowel sound is repeated. In a sense, a slant rhyme is simply a form of consonance or assonance.

Rhyme schemes are denoted by means of lowercase letters, so that rhyming couplets would be marked as *aabb...*, a four-line enveloped stanza would be *abba cddc effe...*, and an Italian sonnet would be *abbaabba cdecde*. Place these letters in the right hand margin of the text, as a working tool. See the Shakespeare quote below for an example of this notational form.

Scansion is based on metrical analysis of a poem and is a convenient shorthand for marking the meter of a poem, especially when you suspect that the poet is making a conscious use of metrical structure. An unstressed syllable is marked with a (ˇ), and a stressed one with a (´). The spondaic measure, which is analogous to a full stop in music, is marked with a —. The scansion for the following lines from *The Tempest* reveals that although he is fluid and relaxed in his placement of line breaks, he nevertheless adheres closely to a pattern of iambic tetrameter and rhyming couplets:

Let me not,	c
Since I have my dukedom got	c
And pardon'd the deceiver, dwell	d
In this bare island by your spell;	d
But release me from my bands	e
With the help of your good hands.	e
Gentle breath of yours my sails	f
Must fill, or else my project fails,	f
Which was to please.	

Simile is used by the poet to make explicit a particular likeness between two things, or between an idea and a thing. "Your love is like a yo-yo" is a simile which directs the reader's attention to the likeness between the abstraction, love, and a concrete, easily pictured object, the common yo-yo.

Spatial Couplet - see Page Layout

Stanzas are used by poets to organize their language in the way that writers of prose use paragraphs. Stanzas are separated by a line space, and repeat some pattern of rhyming such as *abba cddc...*, or *aba bcb cdc....* Stanzas can also be unrhymed, and can be, like spatial couplets, organized by their placement on the page: Frank O'Hara's poems (pg. 88 and 102) are good examples of this strategy.

Traditional Forms are numerous. A few that appear in *Talking Back To Poems* are Terza Rima (Ciardi, pg. 80, rhyme scheme: *aba bcb cdc ded eae aaa*); Ottava Rima (Lord Byron, pg. 78, rhyme scheme: *abababcc*); Sonnet (Wordsworth, pg. 82, rhyme scheme: *abbaabbacdcdcd*).

Appendix

THE WRITING PROCESS

Step 1 Write words or picture-ideas on blank paper, circle and connect them as they occure to you. Look for relationships. Add bubbles or short lists or any other form of brainstorming or doodling that opens your mind and invites clear thought to wander in. Reach out for ideas and connections. Stand on your head if it helps to stimulate your thinking.

Step 2 To paraphrase a famous by-line, "writing a rough draft is not having to say you're sorry." This means, when you are writing the first copy of an essay or poem, you do not need the added burden of obsessive editing. So do as little editing as possible while writing a rough draft. When you are trying to get thoughts down for the first time, there is enough challenge in simply coordinating mind and hand.

Step 3 Like the banal paraphrase above, much that is sorry can be cleared away and what is said will be healthier. Revising for meaning broadly describes the "crow-bar and hammer" part of the process, ripping out words and phrases, trimming off unneeded verbiage, nailing them back where they are more to the point. This is where you strive to write in less obtrusive and more transparent prose or poetry. Any time that you have revised for clarity of thought, you should have a huge scrap heap of ineffective words and misconstrued pieces of syntax.

Step 4 The last step is where pride of workmanship and consideration for your reader comes to the fore. It is a willful act of attention to the nagging details that ought not to matter, except that every flaw of grammar, every blemished spelling, and every skewed preposition distracts the reader from what you are saying. It is precisely because you want your "text" to be transparent to the reader that you become a devotee of conventional standards of usage. When you write a poem, of course, you may ignore any convention if it creates the effect you are after.

Bibliography

Brooks, Jr., Cleanth and Warren, Robert Penn. *Understanding Poetry: An Anthology For College Students.* New York, 1938. This book is in its umpteenth edition for a very good reason: it stands ever ready to yield insight. It can be idly dipped into for years and years of poetic reward.

Ciardi, John. *How does a Poem Mean?* Boston, 1959. This collection of essays is challenging, but extremely useful. The essay on Lewis Carroll entitled "A Burble Through the Tulgey Wood" is a primary source for the thinking that evolved into *Talking Back To Poems.*

Cole, William, ed. *Eight Lines and Under: An Anthology of Short, Short Poems.* New York, 1967. E.B. White once wrote that he hated any poem that wasn't a short poem. William Cole understands this and edits a collection of brilliant gems:

Must
All this aching
Go to making
Dust?

～ *Alun Lewis*

Short poems also tend to make good Talk Back poems. I recommend *Eight Lines and Under* if you are looking for more poems to which you can talk back.

Deutsch, Babette. *Poetry Handbook: A Dictionary of Terms.* New York, 1962. This is the single best source for basic understanding of key words: think of it as an extended glossary of language about poetry.

Kennedy, X.J. and Kennedy, Dorothy M. *Knock At A Star: A Child's Introduction To Poetry.* Boston, 1982. If you are coming at poetry from a child's point of view (and I always try to), this is a very nice place to start.

Mayes, Frances. *The Discovery Of Poetry.* New York, 1987. Mayes anthology is modelled on the one by Warren and Brooks, but includes mostly recent American poetry. There must be a million anthologies of poetry in print today; this is the best one I know about.

Miles, Josephine, ed. *The Ways of the Poem.* Englewood Cliffs, 1961. I don't know anyone who has a finer ear for poetry than Josephine Miles. Her essays introducing each of the five sections of her anthology are well worth reading.

Oliver, Mary. *A Poetry Handbook.* New York, 1994. Oliver is extremely strong and effective in her discussion of sound in poetry. She also offers some support for the imitative aspect of *Talking Back To Poems* when she says, "imitation is a very good way of investigating the real thing."

Williams, Miller. *Patterns of Poetry: An Encyclopedia of Forms.* Baton Rouge, 1986. For a book on the structures of poetry, this is it.

Acknowledgments

"The stone...", Charles Simic.
George Brazillier, Inc.
One Park Avenue
New York, NY 10016

"The Faith," and "Rooter," from *The Collected Poems of Josephine Miles, 1903-83,* copyright © 1983, by Josephine Miles. Used with permission of the University of Illinois Press.

"Piano After War," by Gwendolyn Brooks, copyright © 1991, from her book *Blacks,* published by Third World Press, Chicago, 1991.

"Allegro," Tomas Transtromer, translated by Robert Bly. Reprinted from FRIENDS, YOU DRANK SOME DARKNESS: THREE SWEDISH POETS, translated by Robert Bly, Beacon Press, 1975. Copyright 1975 by Robert Bly. Reprinted with his permission.

"Note," and "Traveling Through The Dark," copyright © 1977 William Stafford, from *Stories That Could Be True* (Harper & Row). Reprinted by permission of The Estate of William Stafford.

"The Oven Bird," and "Mowing," Robert Frost, copyright 1970 by Lesley Frost Ballantine. Holt, Rinehart and Winston, Inc.

"In a Station of the Metro," Ezra Pound, copyright 1971 by Ezra Pound. New Directions Book Publishing Corporation 333 Sixth Avenue New York, NY 10014

"Lovers in Winter," Robert Graves, copyright 1966 by Robert Graves. Reprinted from *Collected Poems* by permission of Collins-Knowlton-Wing, Inc.

"Winter Poem," Nikki Giovanni, copyright 1969 by Nikki Giovanni. *Re:Creation* reprinted by permission of Broadside Press

"Fork," Charles Simic, from *Dismantling The Silence.* George Brazillier, Inc. One Park Avenue New York, NY 10016

"I Was Afraid Of Dying," & "Spring Images" from *The Branch Will Not Break,* copyright © 1963 by James Wright. Wesleyan University Press by permission of the University Press of New England.

"Fidelity," by D.H. Lawrence, from THE COMPLETE POEMS OF D.H. LAWRENCE by D.H. Lawrence, Edited by V. de Sola Pinto & F.W. Roberts. Copyright © 1964, 1971 by Angelo Ravagli and C.M. Weekley, Executors of the Estate of Frieda Lawrence Ravagli. Used by permission of Viking Penguin, a division of Penguin Books USA Inc.

"To Waken An Old Lady," William Carlos Williams, copyright 1944 by William Carlos Williams. New Directions Publishing Corporation.

"Sailing to Byzantium," W.B. Yeats. Reprinted with permission of Simon & Schuster Inc., from THE POEMS OF W.B. YEATS: A NEW EDITION edited by Richard J. Finneran. Copyright © 1928 by the Macmillan Publishing Company, renewed 1956 by Georgie Yeats.

"The Hollow Men," from COLLECTED POEMS 1909-1962 by T.S. Eliot, copyright 1936 by Harcourt Brace and Company, copyright © 1964, 1963 by T. S. Eliot, reprinted by permission of the publisher.

"Orpheus 7," Translated by
Babette Deutsch, copyright 1969 by
Babette Deutsch from *The Collected
Poems of Babette Deutsch,*
Doubleday & Company, Inc.

"Youth and Age," W.B. Yeats
Reprinted with the permission of Simon
& Schuster, Inc., from THE POEMS OF
W.B. YEATS: A NEW EDITION, edited by
Richard J. Finneran. Copyright © 1928 by
Macmillan Publishing Company,
renewed 1956 by Georgie Yeats.

"Breakfast," Wilfred Gibson
from *Collected Poems 1905-1925,*
reprinted by permission of
Mr. Michael Gibson & Macmillan,
London and Basingstoke

"A Little Poem." Reprinted by permission
of Louisiana State University Press from
IMPERFECT LOVE: Poems by
Miller Williams. Copyright © 1986 by
Miller Williams.

"Eight O'Clock," A.E Housman
from *The Collected Poems of A.E.
Housman.* Copyright 1939, 1940 by
Holt, Rinehard & Winston, Inc.
Copyright © 1967 by Robert E. Symons.
Reprinted by permission of
Henry Holt and Co., Inc.

"IV," "VII," and "IV," e.e. cummings,
copyright 1923, 1962 by
e.e. cummings, copyright 1968 by
Marion Morehouse Cummings from
Complete Poems: 1913-1962.
Harcourt Brace Jovanovich, Inc.
New York

"Men Marry What They Need, I Marry
You," John Ciardi, copyright 1958 by
Rutgers, The State University
Rutgers University Press
New Brunswick, New Jersey

"Castle of Thorns," and "By the Road to
the Air-Base," Yvor Winters,
copyright 1960 by Yvor Winters.
The Swallow Press Inc., Chicago

"Note," William Stafford,
copyright 1960 by William Stafford
from *Stories that Could be True: New and
Selected Poems,* Harper & Row,
Publishers, Inc.

"A Major Work," William Meredith.
From PARTIAL ACCOUNTS by
William Meredith. Copyright © 1987 by
William Meredith. Reprinted by
permission of Alfred A. Knopf, Inc.,
New York

"A Coat," W.B. Yeats. Reprinted with per-
mission of Simon & Schuster Inc., from
THE POEMS OF W.B. YEATS edited by
Richard J. Finneran. Copyright 1983 by
Anne Yeats.

"Autobiographia Literaria," by
Frank O'Hara. Copyright © 1967 by
Maureen Granville-Smith,
Administratrix of the Estate of Frank
O'Hara. Reprinted by permission of
Alfred A. Knopf, Inc.

"Little Exercise," Elizabeth Bishop,
copyright 1967 by Elizabeth Bishop
from *Collected Poems,* Farrar, Straus &
Giroux, New York

"The Harbour," Derek Walcott,
copyright 1968 by Derek Walcott.
Farrar, Straus & Giroux, New York

"After Great Pain," by Emily Dickinson.
Reprinted by permission of the publish-
ers and the Trustees of Amherst College
from THE POEMS OF EMILY DICKINSON,
Thomas H. Johnson, ed., Cambridge,
Mass.: The Belnap Press of Harvard
University Press, Copyright © 1951, 1955,
1979, 1983 by the President and Fellows
of Harvard College.